Oh Krishna, Come Again!

OH KRISHNA, COME AGAIN!

Dinkar Joshi

translated by

V. Viswanath

DIVE IN THE OCEAN OF KNOWLEDGE
Ocean Books

Ocean Books Pvt. Ltd.

ISO 9001:2015 Publishers

Published by
Ocean Books (P) Ltd.
4/19 Asaf Ali Road,
New Delhi-110 002 (INDIA)
e-mail: info@oceanbooks.in

ISBN 978-81-8430-544-9
Oh Krishna, Come Again!
by Shri Dinkar Joshi

Edition
2025

Price
₹ 500.00 (Rupees Five Hundred only)

Printed at
R-Tech Offset Printers, Delhi

Preface

Eructation of Satiate and Insatiate

Shri Krishna has been regarded an as incarnation of the God Almighty. Indeed, for atheists, Shri Krishna is a mere character of Mahabharat, Harivansh, Shrimad Bhagawat, etc. This character is partly historical and partly legendary.

It is an undisputed fact that Shri Krishna in all his versions – whether as incarnation of God Almighty or as a character of books Mahabharat, Harivansh, Shrimad Bhagawat, etc. – has attracted and enthralled the human kind for times immemorial.

It can hardly be denied that all the authors of the world and all the performing artists do not satiate till the character of Shri Krishna touches them with the sense of divine accomplishment while depicting one or more facets of the life of Shri Krishna.

Confirming Shri Krishna to any precise form, such as, incarnation of the God Almighty or character of legendary volumes, is the result of limited human perception. I have always believed that, in reality, Shri Krishna is nothing but infinite emotion having no precise form but which can be felt eternally.

Insatiable craving in human mind to have something formless is in itself a testimony of human perception of Lord Shri Krishna. Such insatiable longing, however, leaves the human beings' minds lack of sense of fulfillment. While breathing, a shriek comes out automatically – Oh Krishna!

Would you please come once again to have me a sight? I wish to tell you something.

Vasudev, Devaki, Rukmini, Satyabhama, Arjun, Draupadi, Ashvatthama, Akroor and Kansa – all characters more or less associated with Shri Krishna – had the good fortune of having existed with Shri Krishna. Often in our imagination, their discourses and dialogues with Shri Krishna come alive. At times, we feel that all these characters are breathing within us. Therefore, we beseech Shri Krishna, the Lord Almighty to grace us with his sight once again and have a dialogue with us and give us the opportunity to share our feelings for Him!

However, have we ever thought of that should Shri Krishna really visit us, what shall we tell him? Do we have anything worthwhile to share with him? We do not have any answer to these questions. Even then our craving to have a sight of Shri Krishna remains unfulfilled. This is the real tragedy of human life.

Uddhav and Radha never invited Shri Krishna for meeting because they were aware that Shri Krishna was always in their hearts. The moment we realise and understand this perception of Uddhav and Radha, our desire to have a sight of him will stand fulfilled. The search of this perception of Uddhav and Radha about Shri Krishna is the prime element of this novel.

In expressing myself in this sensitive novel, I was inspired mainly by Mahabharat, Harivansh, Shrimad Bhagawat and Vishnupuran. I express my gratitude to ancient scriptures – Agnipuran, Brahma vaivart puran and Padma puran. I also bow in gratitude to stalwarts from Bankimbabu to Karasandas Manek, whose thoughts and works were a great inspiration to me.

This novel was published in 1986-87 in a Gujarati daily newspaper 'Gujarat Samachar'. Thereafter, it was translated in Hindi and serialised in 'Dharmayug'. It was also reprinted in 'Karmveer' and 'Dainik Jagaran'. So far, this novel has been translated in a number of Indian regional languages, viz. Hindi, Marathi, Telugu, Malayalam, Oriya and Bangla.

When I learnt from Swami Sampurnanandji of Aurobindo Ashram, Puducherry that the Sanskrit translation of novel is in progress, I was pleasantly surprised. He also informed me that Swami Vishvanathji had completed the English translation of this novel that was being sent to me for further steps for publication. This was one more pleasant surprise for me.

I am immensely grateful to Swami Sampurnanandji and Swami Vishvanathji for their contribution in translating this novel in Sanskrit and English and, thereby, expanding the reach of this novel to a vast majority of readers spread across different parts of the country. Indeed, the credit for this also goes to my publisher.

This novel has given me immense satisfaction of completing a worthwhile work. If this novel achieves the purpose of touching the heart of the readers, my satisfaction will forever be greater.

— Dinkar Joshi

102-A, Park Avenue
Dahanukarwadi, M.G. Road
Kandivali – (W)
Mumbai 400 067
Phone – 022-28019795
Email – dinkarmjoshi@rediffmail.com
Website – www.dinkarjoshi.com

1

The blazing mid-noon sun turned towards the west. His furious rays left an envelope of depression on the steeples of the golden castles of Dwaraka. In the west, the Raivatak mountain was standing erect, with its tall peak. But its slant shadow was falling on the ground as if portraying the bent forehead of Raivatak. From somewhere far, the sound of the lashing waves of the ocean could be heard. On the right, some cows grazing in the green fields, hearing the sound of horse-trots, they slightly opened their eyes, and started flapping their ears and tails. They had stopped chewing the cud. The path on the left of Raivatak was moving toward the southern horizon, touching the mountain's shadow. By the sand-mount being raised by the moving chariot, the marks left by the horse-hooves and foot prints of pedestrians were getting covered and erased.

Pulling the reins of the trotting horses with his right hand, Daaruk raised his brows towards Raivatak. White froth started flowing from the mouths of the panting horses. The chariot slowed down a bit.

"O Paarth!", Daaruk drew the attention of Arjuna, sitting at the back in a near-trance-like manner, saying, "we have reached within eye-distance of the Raivatak".

It was as if Arjuna did not even hear Daaruk's words. He sat staring at the Raivatak with unblinking eyes. All of a sudden the closed fist grasping the Gaandeev kept on his shoulder, became soaked with sweat. Was it not the same Raivatak from over whose slanting ramp he had kidnapped Subhadra? Krishna himself had told him, "Arjuna, this is my younger sister Subhadra. If you wish to marry her then you kidnap her. Kidnapping a maiden for marrying her, is not forbidden for Kshatriyas".

Thus, Arjuna's eyes were cocked up, as though Krishna's voice was echoing even today. "What was righteous, and what was unrighteous"—Krishna would constantly keep instructing him all this... Today...

His entire body was bathed in sweat. Even then, how much burning was there in the skin? The manner in which his limbs had wilted, throat parched on the field of Kurukshetra 36 years ago;...! He felt his body being squeezed even today, exactly that way...!

"Kaunteya!" Daaruk interrupted his trance once again, saying, "Water from the ocean has started filling up in the eastern moat of the castle. We will be able to enter only from the western gate".

There was no reaction on Arjuna. What difference did it make whether the chariot entered from the western gate into Dwaraka, or from the eastern gate? What use of such entry into Dwaraka without Krishna? Arjuna had never ever imagined such a thing...! That the Dwaraka into which he would place his feet in a few moments was devoid of Krishna now...! Balaram was not there. Saatyaki was not there. Pradyumna or Aniruddha were not there. And, Uddhav and Akroor were also not there...

If all these people are not there, then how is this desolate township still there? Spread out in 12 *Yojanas* (96 miles), this piece of land was a field full of *kusha* grass, not Dwaraka. It was Krishna himself who transformed this *kusha*-grass land into Dwaraka. It had appeared as if this piece of land was standing holding the finger of the Raivatak mountain.

Once again Arjuna's eyes stood staring towards the direction of Raivatak. This time he did not remember Subhadra also. It felt as if some lilting music was descending from heaven mingling with the air. That music...

It is same tune which the Satepoch King Raivat and his daughter had heard in the musical congregation of Brahmaaji. Treta Epoch had long been completed, now even Dwapara Epoch was about to come to an end. The end of Krishna's bodily-sojourn indicates the end of a complete Epoch. Was it indeed the same music of heaven that was resounding on the peaks of Raivatak, even at the end of Dwapara Epoch?

Or...!...was it the flute of Krishna that he had heard?

Suddenly, Arjuna felt—How accursed am I? Even after having spent so many years with him, I had not heard the sound of the flute coming from Krishna's lips. Sitting on the branch of the Kadamba tree or standing beside the waters of Kalindi when Krishna must have placed the flute on his lips, at that time perhaps he himself manifested as divine-music...!

Arjuna had lived alongside with all the Krishnas, i.e. the Krishna of Indraprasth, Krishna of Hastinapur, Krishna of Dwaraka... But with the Krishna of Vrajabhoomi? That Krishna, simply remained in his imagination, isn't it? He had the vision of the manifestation of Krishna on the battle-field of Kurkshetra. It is true that all the universes were included in this form; but even in that form, the music of that flute was not heard, isn't it?

"Indeed...! How could it have been heard?"—Arjun mused, "If at all the music of the flute could have been heard amidst the tumult of conches and kettle-drums, then how could this total destruction have ever taken place? And, if at all this total destruction could have been prevented!, ... then after 36 years, this quarrel among the Yadavas would also not have taken place. All this is indeed the outcome of the curse given by Mother Gaandhari regarding the annihilation of the Vrishni-clan.

"Dhananjay"...! Daaruk drew the attention of Arjuna third time, "It appears as if these horses are not willing to tread over Dwaraka. Behold...behold...!"

What Daaruk said was indeed true. Why were Daaruk's obedient horses disobeying him today? Neighing fast, both the horses kicked up their all four front legs high into the air. The chariot tilted a little towards the back, and Arjuna taking support of the chariot managed to balance himself.

"Daaruk! How can I to place my feet in a Dwaraka devoid of Krishna? How can I look at that mansion where Krishna lived? O Daaruk… Daaruk…, you return back with the chariot, O brother!"

No doubt Arjuna uttered these tear-soaked words, but tears did not burst out...! because today the reins of his chariot were not in the hands of Krishna. In his place sat Daaruk.

"These grandfathers, these acharyas, these brothers, these sons-grandsons, sons-in-law, relatives! I will not fight with all of them—I cannot strike at them…" …saying so, … it was indeed easy for him to cast aside his Gandeev and sit desolately amidst the 18 *Akshauhini* army because, then the reins of the chariot was in the hands of Krishna…! Krishna was there to take care of it. At that time, what tension did Arjuna have at all...?

But today! How much everything had changed! Then Arjuna's charioteer was Krishna; today Krishna's charioteer was driving Arjuna's chariot. That charioteer who might have transported Krishna hither and thither... that very charioteer, cannot now transport Arjuna anywhere. Arjuna suppressed within himself, the fierce ocean-of-woefulness wailing up inside...! This suffering cannot now become any big manifestation worthy of being viewed, because, where is Krishna now to uplift it to new heights, and give a new twist to its meaning...? This suffering today, which Krishna had earlier on the battlefield derided as unmanliness... would, merely become derived into cowardness. Alas! If only Krishna had even an inkling, that it is that very, unmanliness which has returned once more, and has encompassed Arjuna today...?

Arjuna suddenly became alert. Amidst the deep lines of suffering on his face, lines of shame also surfaced up...! Krishna would never hold the reins of the chariot of a valourless Arjuna. Krishna would never cheer-up a weak-hearted Arjuna.

"Daaruk!", for the first time Arjun addressed, "Horses do not have words, but certainly it is not as if they do not have feelings also, isn't it? Halt the chariot for a while, Daaruk, and, caressing the backs of the horses, go...go… and console them"…

Daaruk halted the chariot. The horses neighed a little once again. Getting down Daaruk placed his hands on their backs. Their tender skin slightly trembled. Daaruk slowly patted their backs. Embracing their necks, he rested his head on their bodies. The eyes of the horses became wet as if with shame, seeing this pitiable plight of Daaruk. Arjuna was watching all this with unblinking eyes.

"O Cherished ones", said Daaruk, as if he was saying this in their ears, "Krishna himself could not reverse the decision of destiny that is why he himself yielded to time eternal. Now that very same destiny wishes to get some residual deeds done through us. O sons, we cannot turn our backs from becoming the instruments of It's wishes.! Come, let us obey the guiding fingers of destiny...!"

The horses neighed as if they understood everything! Daaruk again took up the reins. The chariot turned slightly towards the west. The western gates of the mansion were already lying open. The chariot had already come under the sight of the sentries deployed on the rampart. They lightly played the instruments hanging at the rampart, and its sound filled the atmosphere with its reverberations. The sentries standing below also becoming alert, cast their eyes around. The fluttering of the chariot's flag with its shining symbol appeared to sound louder than even the rumbling sound of the chariot. The chariot approached near. The sentries with their heads bowed down in respect recognized Daaruk and Arjuna. Lowering their weapons, they silently welcomed the charioteer and its occupant. Daaruk turned around and looked at Arjuna. Arjuna was filling his blank eyes with the vision of a Dwaraka, appearing in front of him like a dried up autumn-tree...!

Indeed this was the very same Dwaraka, the windows and towers of whose houses would be decorated with festoons strung with Ashoka and Mango leaves. There would not be even a single compound whose front-yard would be left without being decorated with fresh *Rangolis* (colourful designs drawn). Flower-filled gardens with their water-sprinkled groves and creepers, would be filling the atmosphere with their exhilarating-intoxicating fragrance. Today they all seemed like some far away lack-lustre memories. Few dried-up festoons were seen hanging, with some in which the leaves had faded, and some mere 'dead-snake-like strings' hanging could be seen…!

The *yajna-kunds* (sacrificial-moulds) were seen strewn with heaps of ashes in them. Somewhere from the house of some elderly Dwaraka-resident, the hazy-smoke arising from the oblation offered into a *yajna-kund* could be seen rising up! In the open space devoid of *Rangolis*, signs of some blurred twinkling of old *Rangoli*-powder could be seen. The golden steeples on the houses of Krishna, Balaram, Saatyaki, and Vasudev, were trying vainly to reflect back the radiance of the setting-sun. The Royal-roads would normally be throbbing with life! today...on both sides of these roads, crowds of males-and-females could be seen looking at Arjuna with forlorn eyes…and would then bow down their necks, as though their entire consciousness had dried up...! Worn out faces, worn-out eyes on those family-symbols, stood as if they not had bath for months…! and with their unchanged clothes, those faces could be seen moving around.

"Daaruk...!"...Arjun's lips trembled, saying, "This... This... Is this truly Dwaraka? O brother! or, is it by mistake you brought me to some other township?"...

"Paarth...!", Daaruk said without turning back, "This is the remnants of the bodies left behind after the life-force of their Souls has left! This indeed...! is the recognizable forms of those remaining people..."

It was as if Daaruk's words had dissolved into nowhere...! A long-familiar solemn voice was resonating in Arjuna's ears—"This Soul, which weapons cannot cleave, which fire cannot burn, which wind cannot dry, and which water cannot wet, is indestructible, O Arjuna!"...

Who had said this? Whose voice was it? It was indeed Krishna who had said this to Arjuna 36 years ago. When the Gandeev had slipped out of his hands, and to the sweat-soaked Arjuna,...it was indeed Krishna who had explained about this immortality of the Soul...! "Where is that immortality now today?"

But how is Krishna's Soul? He is some Supreme principle beyond even Soul...! Soul could be of Arjuna, of Daaruk, or of the chariot-pulling horses; But Krishna's...? Was he merely an "Soul"? That principle also had become invisible now, and on the eve of becoming invisible, had commanded Daaruk—"You return to Hastinapur and inform Arjuna about this and bring him here. On my behalf you assign Arjuna the responsibility of looking after Dwaraka, after me, O brother...! Convey my bows to both father Vasudev and Devaki."

Daaruk heard the command of Krishna, and diverted his eyes away from Dwaraka. Today, obeying that very same command he was returning. That Dwaraka which he had left behind, was not this Dwaraka. It was indeed Arjuna who was sitting behind in the chariot, but Dwaraka appeared like some accursed-lifeless townhip...!

"Daaruk", Arjuna said, "Take the chariot to the revered Vasudeva's residence first."

Quietly Daaruk turned the chariot towards Vasudeva's residence. Many townsfolk were standing on the towers, balconies and quadrangles of the desolate township. The whole township appeared so paralysed, that even their breathing seemed to resonate...!

The sentries of the mansions kept their weapons down and bowed their heads. Even before Daaruk could halt the chariot—as if reading the wishes of both occupants—the horses stood up by themselves. Arjuna was to get down, but he remained standing, taking support of Gandeev. In a short while from now, he would meet Vasudeva—a very old and revered personage; and then mother Devaki—who had renounced him no sooner she gave birth—...! had to renounce!—that son, that-Epoch-personage, who left her in the twilight of her life. When Arjuna will now do bow to the unfortunate father of this grand soul", then...?

"Krishna…O Krishna…!" it was as though Arjuna was shrieking out—! "On the last day of the Mahabharat war, if only you had got down first from the chariot, from which you made me get down first...! ...then this difficult moment would not have presented itself before me today...! The already flared-up chariot due to the onslaught of arrows on it, would have then turned into ashes within the wink of an eye...! And…and…if only I also had become! rending the heart into pieces, this…this suffocating moment…would not have arisen…!

But that moment was already there!

□

2

If at all there was a state beyond old age, then Vasudev and Devaki were sliding into that state or else...that state had completely enveloped them.... They had not crossed the boundaries of Dwaraka since many years. Their beings were still cherishing their breaths, even as their emaciated limbs were trapped in a rusty cage, that heart was still pulsating... in which the memory of the journey from Gokul to Mathura carrying the basket with baby-Krishna in it...was throbbing! Even as he had waded through the overflowing waters of the flooded Kalindi river gushing forth with the torrential rains. That brutal scene of eight babies being dashed against the rock by Kansa's hands had not dimmed even in this decrepit state....

Hearing the trots of horses, Vasudeva's worn out eyes became a bit alert. What all had they not seen? And what remained worthy of being seen now?! Sons, grandsons, great-grandsons, brothers, nephews, brothers-in-law.... No one was left now among these.... Even Krishna and Balaram themselves had left them behind. Now, Vajra the one and only great-grandson of Aniruddha was left, an innocent teenager...!

Krishna himself had come and narrated about the quarrel of the Yadavas which had taken place in the designated place called Prabhas-Kshetra, to his father, "Revered father! Elder Brother Balaram has prepared himself into a meditative-state on the shores of the sea, prior to his final departure. Mother Gandhari's curse has started fructifying. Andhak, Vrishni, Bhojak—and, the entire Yadav clan have become victims of their own deeds. This Dwaraka no longer remains to be my dwelling-place, O father...! Please relieve me from Dwaraka O father...! I cannot stay back in Dwaraka any longer now...!"

For the last time, Vasudeva stroked the head of his son, and caressed his cheeks, with shivering hands. Devaki lovingly stroked the back of her son, who was prostrating in front of her. Alas...! they were all under the mercy of eternal time—the time and deeds are always pre-determined!

"You are indeed the personification of Dharma, son...!" Father had asked his son the question, "Tell me, am I the only unfortunate one, to whom the Rishi of the Vedic-times had given the boon,…and have been deprived of it?"

"Which boon, O father...?", Krishna asked looking at his father.

"That those who descend after me may never depart before me; this is the boon that the Vedic-times Rishi had asked. Alas...! Right from the beginning I have been deprived of this boon. The pain which is arising today from it, had never ever before been experienced, O Krishna!"

Vasudeva's voice choked. After composing himself a bit, he kissed the forehead of his son softly, and then closed his eyes…. When he opened his eyes after a moment, there was no Krishna to be seen anywhere in the arena...!

When Arjuna had entered Vasudeva's compound, his eyes were focused on the door itself. Ever since the time Daaruk had left for Hastinapur, since then, Vasudeva and Devaki had accepted this self-imposed imprisonment within their compound, on themselves. Vasudeva was eagerly awaiting the arrival of Arjuna. Krishna himself had said while departing, "Arjuna will come here, revered father! He will set-up the required worthy future order for the remaining clansmen, O father...! You start seeing Krishna in Arjuna from now onwards...!"

Vasudeva and Devaki, were both right in front now...! Arjuna hesitated at the door a while. His eyes had stiffened, as if dazed. He had already accepted the bitter truth about the inevitability of old-age. He was himself a victim of this sequel of old-age.... Where had Krishna himself remained a youth? But not this state of old-age...! Old-age was oozing out of every hair-pore...! This appearance was completely new...! Vasudeva and Devaki never appeared so old. Suddenly, Arjuna woke up out of his reverie, into the present. Quickly moving forward, he prostrated at the feet of Vasudeva and Devaki.

"Revered Father...!"...he couldn't utter anything further....

"Who is it? Arjuna? At last you arrived son!" ...Vasudeva placed his trembling hands on his head, "Did you not bring Krishna with you? And where is Balaram? Pradyumna, Aniruddha, Satyaki. No one else is also seen...!"

Arjuna shivered...he turned towards Daaruk standing at the door...Daaruk slowly moved away from there.

"Revered father...!" Seating himself on the carpet near Vasudeva, Arjuna said, "Please compose yourself father...! From now on we will not see Krishna in any one form or in any one place. But what does it matter? Krishna is with us...is present in every atom of our existence...he is still alive amidst us, O father...!" Then turning his face toward Devaki he said, "Mother! You are the one who gave birth to Krishna...."

"Yes son! But what a unlucky Mother I am"....

"How can Krishna's mother be unlucky, Mother?"

"Which mother in the world would have sent the child that had come out her womb, to another house without even breast-feeding it, or holding it to her bosom?!... Who can be there like that mother, O son? The mother, with whose bosom her child had never ever cuddled, that-mother!..."... Devaki's voice refused to co-operate with her....

"Mother, it is well known about the pampering-way in which your son was brought up in the lap of mother Yashoda...."

"In that case Paarth, why did I not become Yashoda instead of Devaki? I did not feed him his most favourite butter and sweets with my hands, isn't it?! I did not get the fortune of placing him on my lap and patting him to sleep, isn't it?" Devaki burst out into tears....

"Please don't say like that, Mother", Arjuna consoled her saying, "You are the mother of a Epoch Personage like Krishna...! in order to eat the butter and sweets only from your hands, Krishna will have to return once more, mother!"

"Arjuna!", exclaimed Devaki, after feeling somewhat consoled, and said, "Once I had strongly insisted on feeding Krishna butter and sweets with my hands. But this son of mine, travelling to Hastinapur, Indraprasth, Mathura, Pragjyotishpur, and all over the entire Aryavart, would get very little time to sit peacefully. If at all I had caught him calm and steady in one place, I had invited him to come to this very house of mine to eat food prepared lovingly with my hands. Dear, I had heard a lot about his favourite butter and sweets, that is why I had served those favourite dishes of his...."

"OK mother, ...then...then...what happened mother?", Arjuna interrupted eagerly.

Pointing her shivering finger at a spot, Devaki said,

"This very spot, my son, look at this spot in this very room."

She said, "Seating him here, I had placed the food-plate in front of him...." Devaki had a hard time holding back her hiccup-filled tears, and continued, "He kept staring at the plate, and then, I saw tears in his eyes...! He did not even touch the butter and sweets...and lowered his head...!"

"What are you saying, Mother? Tears in the eyes of Krishna!", said Arjuna and stood as if stunned.

"Yes", said Devaki...patting his head I asked him,— 'Son! What sin has this your luckless mother's hands have done, that instead of eating your favourite butter-sweets served by her, you are sitting crying?'..."

"And…and…Kaunteya...!", she wailed, "do you know what Krishna said?"

He said, "Mother! When I was leaving Gokul and going towards Mathura, at that time I had given mother Yashoda promise saying, 'Mother! I will return again to you… and till I return to you I will not eat my favourite butter and sweets'...."

"And now Mother...!" he said, "on the other hand, this love served with your hands…. O Mother! you only tell me!…this son of two mothers!…in what horns of a dilemma am I caught up? "

Suddenly, Arjuna asked with childlike curiosity, "O Mother...! Then? What did Krishna do then?"

Krishna did only that which he was expected of him to do. My love had sprung up out of my selfishness. The promise given to Yashoda was not out of selfishness, but had manifested out of sacrifice. The love out of sacrifice is always superior...!" Uttering this much, Devaki collapsed,… and lay down helplessly over the pillow. "Now…now…I will never be able to feed my darling butter and sweets out of my hands, Arjuna...never…! If at all you meet Krishna somewhere, please tell her, "Son...Devaki is waiting for you…."

Arjuna stood as if stunned. His heart was as if drooped down…. It seemed as if these words of Devaki… "Devaki is waiting for you…" were resounding back from all sides—!

Arjuna now turned toward Vasudeva;…it was difficult to know if Vasudeva's eyes were wet or dry; because they had sunk into some deep abyss. Whether he had heard even a single word of the entire dialogue between Devaki and Arjuna? ...it was difficult to gauge...!

"Revered father", he softly addressed him.

"Arjuna!", Vasudeva spoke as if he had just woken up. His eyes were lost in something far away…in something beyond…! "The day Krishna released us from the jail of Kansa and for the first time touched my feet, that very moment, son, I have not forgotten even today. For a long, long time, my mind was not willing to acknowledge that… that wondrous delicate child whom I had stealthily left at Gokul on that heavily clouded thundering rainy-night and returned,…that very child having killed Kansa, is standing with his head bent down at my feet...! And it was indeed Krishna...! After complete 14 years, I was seeing Krishna… complete 14 years…! And, and…how, how?…were those 14 years?"

It was now becoming too much for Arjuna to bear. He diverted the topic, "O revered father! the difficult days of imprisonment are long passed now, isn't it? After that he brought you and bestowed upon you the title of Grandsire of the Republic of Mathura and kingdom of Dwaraka…!"

"Yes Dhananjaya! what you say is right; but, the one who released me from imprisonment, O son, he himself has also now given this new imprisonment...!"

"I don't understand...!", Arjuna fell into a quandary.

A dejected smile appeared on Vasudeva's face. Arjuna kept staring. A smile even at this instant?

"The 14 years of imprisonment were one of anticipation, O son!" Vasudeva said, "Krishna is growing up in Gokul, and it is from him that this hope was also growing, that he will release Mathura from the cruel rule of Kansa. The death of Putana, the killing of Dhenukasur,…all this news was reaching my ears, and one felt, that one day most certainly he will reach here also...! The wailing wind blowing outside, the spluttering trees outside the jail—the flapping of the leaves of the creepers, my breathing would become heavy, all sounds could be heard…as if saying, "There he is! Krishna has arrived at laaast...!" Sometimes when the gong struck at mid-night one would feel, 'Is it Krishna knocking at the door?'..."

"Father...!" Arjuna's lips quivered.

"Yes, in that jail in Mathura, there was anticipation...! These days in the jail will pass away…was that not the confidence? Narada had said, 'O Arjuna, Krishna will come...! Devaki's eighth progeny will free Mathura'.... But…but…now Arjuna", said Vasudava, "even some stray word from Narada is also not there to hold on to. In that jail, devoid of Krishna, our life was in our anticipation of Krishna…." Now…now…even that anticipation is not there...! O Arjuna, this imprisonment which we are experiencing today, is more torturous, more agonizing than the confinement in Kansa'a jail."

"Enough…enough, father…! please stop. I can't hear any more...! My heart is broken and bleeding away, O father...!"

"O Paartha...!", Vasudeva said in a low voice, "Now that there is no question of waiting for Krishna, there is only one way to attain freedom from this new jail…." Vasudeva stuttered a while, "That day, I, Krishna's father myself had taken him out of the jail…. Yes, it is indeed true, that we had deprived Krishna of his parents…! And, now, now...! …depriving us of a son!" "Arjuna, it is as if he had whispered in our ears…. 'O father…! those years of agony which I experienced, may both of you also experience a little of that agony…!' O Arjuna…Arjuna,…O son…!" Vasudeva broke down shattered. It was now impossible for Arjuna to stand there anymore. Suddenly, he moved away saying, "O father...! Please grant me permission...! May I go and visit Devi Rukimini and Satyabhama's mansion also, and return? The first twilight of night has begun…."

"Oh...! OK son, go son, go and console Satyabhama and Rukimini also. And…and…", said Vasudeva, "please come back here by the first rays of the early morning sun!"

"Early-morning? Any special purpose?"

"Purpose?" Vasudeva suppressed a faded laugh, "That imprisonment from which there is no hope of getting freedom, the moment of getting freedom from that imprisonment is drawing close…."

"Meaning?"…

"Tomorrow during the very early dawn I shall take Yoga-contemplation, O Arjuna...! This five elemental body has lasted quite long...! Now let these five elements attain a good end...!"

"O father…!"

"After completing the last-rites of my earthly body, you proceed to the Prabhas-kshetra, son! And if at all anywhere near the shores of the deer forest you meet Krishna, tell him that father Vasudeva…."

"And mother Devaki too…" Devaki intervened in the middle and said.

Tell him, "Even in the imprisonment of Heaven, we are waiting for you, O Son...! Tell him that the place where Krishna is not there, that place also is not Heaven for his parents, it is a prison only...! We shall wait for Krishna…till many…many aeons…."

That's all...! What he had suppressed with great difficulty, now broke out in the form of bursting-tears...! He did not want to cry, but Arjuna burst out crying….

□

3

After leaving Vasudeva's mansion, when Arjuna reached the inner-chambers of Krishna's mansion, the night's darkness had already spread. With medium flamed lanterns and wavering flame torches burning here and there, the shadows of Dwaraka looked eerie...! Even at the doorways of the inner chambers there were burning torches and amidst them stood some sentries. With bowed heads they greeted him. Arjuna entered inside. Not even a single corner of those inner chambers of Krishna was unknown to Arjuna. Arjuna had visited this residence of Satyabhama and Rukimini many a time. But today's this arrival…? these inner-chambers…? Today they were completely different...! The garden was lying deserted…. It looked as if for many days no one had watered it.... Here and there heaps of dried leaves had fallen…. Other than the wind, no one was even sweeping them…!

Arjuna recoiled near the stairway. How shall I be able to climb so high? Even while climbing the unapproachable heights of the Himalayas fighting the tribals, he had not even felt anything...! But today, these steps appeared even more unapproachable to him. But alas...! He cannot stand there forever...! Arjuna girdled up his loins and started climbing the stairs. There was light inside, but it was not as if to welcome someone. Leaning against a single pillar in the passage-way, those two queens appeared as if they were dissolving in the darkness. Both of them saw Arjuna coming up the stairs, both of them could understand the anguish in Arjuna's mind, and suddenly Arjuna's plight brought about tears flowing down their eyes.

"You have come, Dhanajaya...!" Moving a little forward, Rukimini steadied Arjuna, "Daaruk had told us that you have arrived.... Since then we have been waiting for you...".

"Please accept my salutations, Devi...!" Arjuna first paid obeisance to Rukimini and then to Satyabhama.

"May you become famous, O Brother...!"

"What kind of blessing is this, Devi? What such work is pending, worth becoming famous for? Where Krishna is not, what fame there?!" said Arjuna.

"Yes indeed...! What fame without Krishna?" Rukimini said, "Arjuna, not merely to the Yadava clan, but the entire Aaryavart has been enveloped by some gruesome sin...! Who knows, result of whose sins this is?"...Rukimini burst out into tears.

"Sister...!"...wiping her own tears and supporting her weeping sister Rukimini, Satyabhama intervened in between, and said, "I...I...had indeed, given such pain to Krishna...! Yes, I am the one guilty.... But O Krishna...! Please...please...tell me, why are you punishing the entire Dwaraka for this sin of mine. Why? Why?"

"What is this you are saying, Satyabhama?" said Arjuna, falling into a dilemma.... "You?...and You? and offend Krishna? How is this possible?"

"Yes Arjuna! Only I becoming a victim of the natural jealousy of women, I had given pain to Krishna. All of us are now suffering the consequences of that very evil deed of mine...!" Satyabhama said, "Krishna should have given only me the punishment for my evil deed!... How? how...could he thus renounce the entire Yadava clan and the township of Dwaraka?" She was unable to stand... Satyabhama suddenly becoming weak, literally slid down. Rukimini stood looking on with wonder...she gently caressed Satyabhama's forehead.

"Sister...!" said Rukimini, "You have become a little too much emotional...!"

"This emotion is endless...O Arjuna!... That spear which is now pricking in my heart, that incident is now becoming too heavy for me to bear.... At least by accepting that sin of mine, let me experience a little relief, O Arjuna..." wailed Satyabhama. Rukimini's hands kept caressing her for a long time. Arjuna sat at the feet of Satyabhama like some robot... he was just staring into void...!

"What I am saying is correct. Yes, Absolutely right. I...I only gave sadness to Krishna.... And the saddened Shyam has turned his face away. O sister Rukimini...! The brave Gudakesh...! That day...that day...!" Satyabhama's upward gazing eyes, slipped somewhere high, deep into some cimmerian darkness in the sky...!

The advent of the Devarishi Narada is always sudden—without any prior indication—this was indeed the routine of Narada. One morning, after completing his morning ablutions, Krishna was sitting relaxed in his residence, when the chimes of Narada's veena could be heard. Getting up, Krishna welcomed the Devarishi, and offered him an appropriate seat. Washing his feet, and then seating himself on a lower seat below Narada, Krishna did bows to him saying—"O Devarishi Narada! You have solemnized this land of Dwaraka after a long time...!"

"O Achyuta...!" said Narada, "Wandering around the Himalayas, I lost track of the days that passed by. I have just returned from the tour of Kailas...."

"It is indeed our good fortune, O Narada...!"...we shall also become blessed by receiving the Prasad from Kailas...."

"Krishna...!" removing a fresh flower from one corner of his upper garment and handing it over to Krishna, Narada said, "This is a Brahmakamal. Plucking it out from the holy waters of Mansarovar in the Kailas-mountains, and after offering it at the feet of Lord Shiva, O Krishna, this flower will ever remain fresh like this."

Krishna, Rukimini, and all others present there, kept gazing at the wondrous flower shining in Narada's hands. Krishna took the Brahmakamal from Narada's hands, touched it to his forehead, and proffering it to Rukimini seated to his left said, "O Rukimini, this flower will beautify your flowing hair. Always adorn your hair with this blessings from Lord Shiva.

Rukimini sat spellbound. Accepting it as a blessing she interlaced it with her hair.

"Really...! O Devi how you are indeed blossoming because of this flower. It seems as if a young daughter of Yaksha is preparing to go out for a stroll into the forest garden." Krishna smiled.

Rukimini felt coy...! Devarishi Narada kept looking smilingly at this delightful and stainless marital relationship. For a long time, spiritual-discussions, general topics, etc., were exchanged between them, and finally everyone departed for their respective rooms.

Krishna himself gave the Brahmakamal given by Narada to Rukimini, and asked her to entwine it within her hair. And not only that, because of the lotus Rukimini appeared to be blooming like a Yaksha-bride…! Satyabhama heard all this, and a rage blazed forth within her. That love, which she had been getting undivided till today, that very love which had reassured Satyabhama, that…although in the royal-assemblage and in the world Rukimini may be the Queen-consort—as far as Krishna's Love-world was concerned, she was the Queen-consort…only she...! Satyabhama...! Till today nothing had happened to jostle this belief of hers...! Today!…today…in front of everyone Krishna expressed his paramount-love towards Rukimini…and acknolwedged it too...! A virtually rare flower like Brahmakamal, Krishna gave it to Rukimini,…not…not…to her...! Satyabhama…!

Such an incident had never occurred so far…! Satyabhama felt that, till today Krishna had been cheating her! Mistaking mere worldly relationship as Love, hope she had not been duped! OK...! Till now what might have been a delusion is all over,...but now…now….this matter will have to be clarified! Hidden standards are not permissible in Love…!"

That day when Krishna came to Satyabhama's mansion, he saw that Satyabhama was lying in a corner, deep inside the innermost-room and crying...! Why? Such a scene was unimaginable to Krishna...! She had completely removed all her ornaments and appeared broken-hearted.

"Satyabhama...!" Krishna called out lovingly, "What is all this going on today? This presentation…and this crying! What such thing has happened that I see tears flowing from your eyes?"

"My delusion is removed today, O Swami...!" Satyabhama said hesitatingly, "For the first I came to know that I have been living under a delusion. I have been a victim of deceit...!"

"What are you saying, O Devi? Who ever has deceived you, has cheated you, he may be in Paatal also, but I shall catch him and bring him before you, and give him whatever punishment you desire to give him."

"No Krishna, no…! you need not take the trouble to catch him. I have been duped not by any anyone else, but at the hands of my whole and soul…. I have been duped by my own Krishna's hands...!"

"Indeed…? You are invoking a very profound problem, O Satyabhama...! I…Krishna…has never cheated anyone… And last of all You…! My dear…."

"Enough...enough...! I have been duped by these very words of yours till today…." …Satyabhama made it very clear and said, "I had all along been thinking that if at all there is anyone dearest of all to Krishna, it is but me... me only…!"

"This is true, O Devi...! Krishna is near to you only…!"

"But O Madhava...! If at all it were so, you would not have given the Brahmakamal to your favourite

Rukimini...." ...Satyabhama uttered those scorpion-sting-like piercing words...!

Krishna understood...! His sky blue countenance got enveloped by a deeper shade of gloom...! What had Satyabhama uttered? How did such envy towards Rukimini ever enter into her bosom? And that too, into the mind of Satyabhama who was ever close to Krishna? from where... where did such impurity enter?

Satyabhama kept silently watching that extremely sad face of Krishna, and started thinking that at last the inner secret of Krishna stood revealed.... She had caught Krishna red handed...! The joy of victory was gleamed on Satyabhama's face...!

"Satyabhama...!" Krishna stood up. Gently touching the shoulder of his wife he said, "You...you...? How did you think thus? I had not even dreamt that a Lotus flower could create such a deep wedge, and that too...in this manner...! If at all I had even an inkling, then I would have consecrated the blessing given by Devarishi Narada back again at Shiva's feet itself."

Satyabhama's eyes remained unblinking...! She had never ever seen such anguish on Krishna's face! Krishna once again remained silent, and did not say anything more. Satyabhama remained wondrously spellbound. Hope unknowingly she had not done injustice towards Krishna! She had never ever seen such an expression on Krishna's face...! Holding on to Krishna's feet, she wanted to seek forgiveness...! But the innate woman ego stopped her from doing so...! Leaving Krishna standing there itself, she went away into the other chamber....

"O Arjuna...!" After a few moments, Satyabhama turned her eyes once again, from where it had strayed away far into the horizon. This time her tone had completely changed—"O Arjuna...! Ever since I defaulted that day, till today a feeling of failure is churning my bosom. Shaking away my ego, if only then...then and there...! I had fallen at Krishna's feet and sought his forgiveness…then perhaps I need not have had to pass through such a heavy mental-agony...!" And all of a sudden she turned her face towards Rukimini, and placed her head at her feet saying, "Please forgive me sister...! That sorrow which I had given Krishna, in that…I had cast a blemish even on you...! All this is only the result of that evil-deed of mine…!"

"Satyabhaaama...!" Arjuna said with great compassion, "Krishna was beyond all human agony. Considering yourself guilty, you are fretting in vain…!

"Yes indeed, sister...!" Rukimini also consoled her.

"Anguish does not enter from somewhere outside, O Arjuna...! This manifests from within itself…. However…!" said Satyabhama, "will you please accept my one prayer, O Brother...?!"

"Command me, O Devi...! Krishna's better-half does not become so pathetic…!"

"If at all Krishna happens to meet you in the Prabhas-region…."

"Satyabhaamaaa...!"

"Indeed, now he shall never return to Dwaraka. These eyes can never see him again because this embodiment is guilty; but who knows may be you do meet Krishna...!"

Arjuna and Rukimini did not respond.

"…. If at all you happen to meet Krishna, do tell him, O Arjuna…Satyabhama is guilty. She made you sad. For that sin please give her as much severe punishment as necessary…but why such a heavy punishment to this entire clan, and to this entire township? Why?…why...? Why did you renounce this? This little plea of mine, O Brother… please convey this to Krishna if possible…" saying…saying thus…embracing Rukimini, she started wailing loudly, and, Rukimini too started crying…!

There was nothing left for Arjuna, except to lose himself unto empty-space...!

□

4

The end of the moment of the second quarter of the night was announced with the sound of the bell's-gong. Its echo was resounding in the atmosphere. As the waters of the sea had almost started filling the moat surrounding the mountain, and the sound arising out of the waves lashing from it, seemed as if knocking at the doors of the night's silence. There was an even deeper silence than that of the silence of this night...in Krishna's mansion. A few burning lanterns, lights in a few prominent chambers,...that's all...! apart from these, everything was completely still...! The sentries at the gates, were standing as if they were lifeless statues. Even their shadows that were seen in the dim moonlight, appeared to be slant, as if conspiring up some secret.

Arjuna was standing by the small skylight window and looking outside—the milky-white stars appeared as if looking down at the universe without any expectations. Krishna is no more there in this world…and…and…. Nature seemed as if she was not at all concerned with all that was happening…Krishna was not there! even then these stars looked as if they were having their mute dialogues. Even when Krishna was there, this mute-dialogue would be going on incessantly..... And now?…now? When Krishna is not there these milky-white stars are totally unconcerned. Probably, these stars that have been shining over such countless universes since time immemorial, have learned to exist by absorbing such voids within themselves...! Probably, similar to this great personage of this Dwapara

Epoch, many such great personages might have manifested in other Epochs also…and, might have also gone away dissolving unto the cycle-of-destiny...!—these…these stars…have been seeing all this arising and dissolving—and…seeing it again and again…! have become immune... stone-like...!

And, in the meantime, a wild meteor had speedily fallen down on earth inscribing a streak of silvery shining light ray behind, and was swallowed up by the darkness. Its light had lit up the dark night. After all! this is but the routine sequence of Nature...! Arjuna's eyes kept roving about in the darkness in search of that meteor.

And now, only the final quarter of night was remaining. Mother Devaki will also bid farewell over the contemplated body of her husband; there was no doubt in that...! In order to convey her message, Krishna will have to be searched out; Satyabhama's message also will have to be conveyed to Krishna. Father Vasudeva,…mother-Devaki,…dearer than life Rukimini…and Satyabhama….—all had full faith… that—no matter what happens. Arjuna will definitely convey their heart rending messages to Krishna...! No one else other than Arjuna could do this task...! After all Krishna's exit has taken place from this elemental-creation, is it not? But…Arjuna…Arjuna…is much beyond this!—he is ever one with Krishna...! Closest to Him…!

But under what a dreadful deception these kinsfolk were living...! Now where is the possibility of Arjuna ever meeting Krishna? After all Arjuna has to maintain his own decorum also...! But whom shall he tell about his this decorum? Because, what benefit will he get by breaking the cord of faith of one who is counting his last moments?

Arjuna was standing all alone in that spacious chamber, caught up in a net of sentiments…all alone...!

This was the same chamber in which he had spent many sweet days with Krishna. In this very same chamber, sitting in different places, many a time, how many things he had told Arjuna…! Now those days…and those things….

In one corner of the chamber, there was a huge stone seat—as if it was meant to be as a big spot for discussions...! On that very seat Krishna's Sudarshan-chakra had been deposited. Now it was not there. Daaruk was telling—

"O Ambidexterous-one...! All the Yadavas had seen that Sudarshan-chakra pervading the entire space surrounding the Prabhas-arena, and then becoming invisible...!" The Yadavas did not understand the significance of the disappearance of the Sudarshan-chakra in this manner!… But…! the Time…the immemorial…! After all It had taken him over...!

Not even any violent power of this world could ever have snatched Krishna's Sudarshan-chakra from his hands...! Krishna himself must have hinted it, to bid farewell...! That which neither the Yadava's nor Daaruk understood, Arjuna was seeing it very clearly...!

"… And…and…Dhananjaya...!" said Daaruk giving him further information, "Out of the contemplated body of Balaram, Sheshnag himself emanated—and that serpent too, after a few moments, seating itself over the waves of the ocean dissolved into it...!…while, the contemplated body of Balaram appeared full of radiance."

All these scenes stood visualized in front of Arjuna's eyes,…as if the huge Sheshnag emanating out of Balaram's body had enveloped all over the entire Prabhas-arena, the entire ocean, and the limitless skies...!

But…but…amidst all this, where is Krishna? He may be still have attained contemplation somewhere in the Prabhas-arena, or else after dropping the body…his five-elements….

Arjuna trembled...!

Arjuna could not bear to see the blank-space devoid of Krishna…he turned away his eyes. There in another corner over a stonepost lay Krishna's dearest Paanchajanya conch. Krishna would always carry it with him….And now…? he left even that and went away. The meaning behind all this was very clear...! Krishna would never ever meet anyone...! Hadn't the body-donning Krishna, become bodiless now?

The gong announcing the arrival of the third quarter of night had sounded. The Brahma-muhoorat was about to begin. For a few moments Arjuna sat cross legged in Padmseat and contemplated upon Brahman. After finishing his bath, etc., he put his offerings into the burning cinder lying inside the yajna-kund; and it was only then…that the first golden rays of the rising sun pierced through the darkness, and showed its crimson face over the Eastern horizon. Arjuna leaned out of the window and looked out…! probably...so early in this darkness Daaruk had not yet arrived…! But…!

Arjuna's doubts proved wrong. Daaruk was standing right there waiting for Arjuna.

"Daaruk...!" Arjuna called out in surprise...!

"Yesss…!…the chariot is ready...!" drawing closer to the window Daaruk said, "The news of grandsire Vasudeva's Yoga-contemplation has spread all over Dwaraka. All the townsmen must be already reaching his mansion."

Arjuna did not give any reply. The meaning of whatever he heard occurred to him—"I shall not be able to have a last vision of grandsire Vasudeva". He told Daaruk, "Quickly take the chariot to the mansion...! Before Pitashri goes into Samadhi, may I be able to once quench my thirst with the nectar-essence flowing from his eyes…and…and then." Deep sighs completed his sentence.

By the time Arjuna reached Vasudeva's mansion, Vasudeva's Soul had already dived deep into some Brahmanaadi within the restless body, waiting to dissolve unto Brahman...!

Where was that Vasudeva, whom Arjuna had seen just now…just seen...just the previous evening...? How radiant and still Vasudeva appeared...! Spreading a tiger-skin, he was seated cross legged on it in Padmseat. Eyes were closed. Some effervescence was seen on the lips. Acknowledging the relationship of epochs to be as if momentary, Mother Devaki was sitting on the left of her husband Vasudeva, with a totally composed demeanor...! It was as if during these last few hours of the night both their bodies had completely changed...!

Taking care that he should not disturb the peace, Arjuna tiptoed and sat in front of Vasudeva. But alas...! Where is Vasudeva now going to open his eyes and see something? Even the slight stirring visible on the lips had started reducing...!

Within a short span of time, Rukimini, Satyabhama, children and countless townsmen gathered in the mansion. Apart from the breathing sound of men, there was no sign of any other sound there...!—There…there was such an intense stillness...! Everyone's eyes were rooted on Vasudeva.

All of a sudden the stirring of his lips stopped. The spacious mansion, as also the countless crowd gathered there,…heard a resonating sound of "Ommmm"…! From where did this sound emanate? Everyone started looking here and there…towards one another...! By the time anyone could surmise anything…once again the resonating sound of "Ommmm" arose...! Now everyone's eyes were rooted on Vasudeva. Not one...! but all of a sudden…it seemed as if countless resonating reverberating-sounds of "Om" had arisen...! Everyone was wonder struck and overwhelmed...! The reverberating intense sound of "Om" was arising from every hair-pore of Vasudeva. Instead of one…thousands of intonations were rippling about in one single intonation in the atmosphere.

And then…then! all of a sudden everything stopped...! Gradually, the resonating "Om" started dwindling…and it slowly became still. The erect body of Vasudeva trundled over on to Devaki's shoulders. Everyone stood as if dumb founded. Effortlessly, the mass intonation of "Om" sprung up from everybody's throats; as if the sound was swimming in the air...!

Amidst the tensed-up kinsmen, Arjuna was the first to become composed. Mother Devaki sat inert as if completely unaware of her husband's motionless-body on her shoulders. Arjuna himself approached near. His hands were also trembling. There was twitching even on his lips. But, what had to be done had to be done…where was any escape from that? Coming near, he gently laid Vasudeva'a body on to the floor.

Till then,…there was nothing except people all over the place! in mansions, gardens, highways,…everywhere, they had squeezed themselves. Although Arjuna viewed this mass of people…he could visualize only a void...! Although there was indeed a mass of people…but...! four Yadavas to give shoulder to father Vasudeva up to the graveyard, could not be sighted anywhere around...! Alas...! The entire Vrishni clan had been destroyed...! For the illustrious father of such great personalities like Krishna and Balaram...! There was no one left from his own lineage to perform his final-rites. There was only one boy-prodigy left...! Taking Vajra the tender teen-aged son of Aniruddha along with him, Arjuna started preparing the body of Vasudeva for his final journey.

The tender rays of the sun kissed the entire earth, and there...!…his own representative Agni's flames, dissolved the terrestrial body of Vasudeva into its five elements. In the very same five elements, Mother Devaki also dissolved herself. It appeared, as if even the wind had forgotten to wipe the tearful eyes of the people around. Even the wind was standing still…listless...! And the rays of the sun was as if fading away fast in order to escape from the intense heat of the funeral pyre...!

Arjuna performed all the rites. He paid attention to everything. After all only he was left...! After finishing all rites, Arjuna called Daaruk—"Daaruk...! The Royal heredity must not be broken, isn't it? Therefore, the only one and only descendant left of the Yadava clan...!"

"Pardon me, O Kaunteya...!" Daaruk interjected in the middle, "It was Father Vasudeva's last wish that you yourself take over the Dwaraka's Royal reign. According to Krishna's command when I proceeded to Hastinapur, at that time Maharaj Vasudeva himself had expressed this very desire…."

"Yes, Arjuna...!"...both queens Rukimini and Satyabhama endorsed Daaruk's statement, "Vajra is still a boy now".

"O Devi, please pardon me", Arjuna explicitly refused, "How can I tell you how I am spending every moment in this Krishnaless Dwaraka…how can I tell you...? "It is impossible for me, O Devi...! I…I seek forgiveness—please permit me...! I cannot delay any further to go to Prabhas-arena and complete the funeral rites of those neglected dead bodies of the brave Yadavas lying scattered all around...! There also I only have to perform...!"

"If that be the case, O Brother", Rukimini said, "It is indeed impossible for us also to remain in this Krishnaless ghost-land Dwaraka…. Whom shall we go and tell, O Arjuna? Take us also to Hastinapur along with you, O Arjuna...!"

"Truly",…the miserable Satyabhama also endorsed, "Our relationship with land has now come to an end...! Just as all relations dissolve unto destiny, are all limited within their respective boundaries...! in the same way—our relationship with this land is also reaching its point of culmination…."

"Daaruk", Arjuna conceded, "If this be the wish of the eminent-ones in this township, then you please make all arrangements. Consulting the elders of the town properly, may their permission also be sought. On the seventh day from today, we shall all proceed towards Hastinapur".

Seventh day?!—Why seven days?—Daaruk did not understand—Why has Arjuna decided on a time-span of seven days? "Now even every single moment seems unbearable, O Paarth...! As soon as possible, let us leave this township…."

"Have you forgotten Daaruk?", Arjuna reminded him, "The work of searching for Krishna in the Prabhas-arena is pending. Krishna's supreme-principle has indeed been freed, but…how can his human-form attain fulfillment, without it being committed to its final rites by me? We shall leave today itself, O Daaruk...! As soon as the third quarter of the day ends…. You proceed to find out from the elders of the township their plans for the future. And, during the fourth quarter, we shall proceed towards the Prabhas-arena…."

Daaruk remained astounded...! Arjuna is able to think for everyone...!

"As you wish, O revered one...!" saying so, Daaruk got up.

After the next quarter, as the sun-rays were spreading across the shadows of Raivatak mountain, Arjuna's chariot was proceeding forward in the direction of the Prabhas-arena. Arjuna had set out in search of something "Unknown"…and…the residents of Dwaraka were engaged in preparing for their Hastinapur journey.

□

5

Splendour is not under the control of expanse and limits...!...that Shiva-temple standing there...! was an incarnate example for this...! During high tide, it seemed as if the sea was coming running till the compound of the temple, to wash the feet of Shiva during high tide. From here it was hardly two or three yojanas remaining to the Prabhas-arena.

As soon as Daaruk saw the flag on the temple, he stopped the chariot.

"Gudakesh...!" he turned and alerted Arjuna, "From here on, the limits of Lord Pinakin's Kaivalya Dham begins. Should we not leave the horses here?"

Ever since the Raivatak mountain's peak had disappeared out of sight, Arjuna had not spoken even a word. Daaruk did try some times, to break his trance silence, but not a sound arose from there.—His eyes were moving all round taking in the skylines from all directions—"Is there something there? If at all he could only get some indication about Krishna...! Where is there some sign which would lead me to Krishna? May there be something by which he could say—This is the message of Vasudeva Devaki Satyab hama...! How many things from others...but his own?! He lost himself somewhere once again—If at all he met Krishna, what personal message did he himself have? And...and may be Krishna might ask also, "Arjuna you have indeed brought others' messages, but what of you? Do you have anything to say?"

To such a likely question by Krishna what answer would he give? Does he not have anything to tell?! But… but…he had lots to tell him...! Indeed...! How many things there were to tell Krishna; but, today? Why is nothing was coming back to his memory? There is no such thing that he had not already told Krishna before this…!

Any footprints of Krishna? Any emblem left behind by him? Nothing was falling within the purview of his sight…! or else was he seeing Krishna himself in each and every footprint that he saw imprinted on the sand? A tune was quivering in the wind which was flowing along with the fluttering leaves of the trees...! Arjuna felt...! This is indeed the intonation of Krishna's flute…! Vibrating...!…then? then?…where is Krishna?

However, it was not proper to take the chariot forward. One has to go barefoot only into the holy place of Lord Pinakin. Arjuna got down from the chariot.

Pointing to a spot within the temple compound, a little higher than the sea shore level, Daaruk said, "O son of Pritha! This is that very spot, from where the plough bearing elder brother's soul had manifested in the form of Sheshanag, and, before disappearing from that spot had dissolved unto the sea."

Arjuna stood spell bound...! He was not sure whether the Gandeev slipped down from his shoulder, or if he had taken it down; but, unwittingly he had done obeisance to that spot, and bent his head low. Even now the remnant ashes from his departed body and his bones were still lying there as it is, in the very spot where elder brother had renounced his earthly body in Samadhi…!

"Daaruk...! This ashes and this remnants of his bones…" Arjuna asked Daaruk.

"Krishna had bid farewell to the earthly body of his elder brother in this very spot. These are still waiting, deprived of the final rituals, O Panadava...!" said Daaruk.

Alas...! There was no one equal to him in the entire Aaryavart...! To such a great person, there was no one left to perform the last rites of his earthly body...! There was not even one son or clansman left to perform the final ritual of this ashes and left-over bones, with a handful of water...!

Arjuna slowly walked up to the sea shore. He slowly wetted his knees in the waves of the sea. Handing over his Royal emblem, Gaandeev, etc., to Daaruk, Arjuna had bath in the sea. With a wet body, facing the west, he performed the Sandhya-ritual; and the offered water on to the final remnants of the Plough wielding elder brother. Cold water flowed over the ashes and the left over bones, and they all got washed away..Now only the memories of Balaram were left behind.

After performing his Sandhya-ritual Arjuna said, "O Daaruk...! Brother, what if we spend our night here itself? This...this...Shiva temple is giving rise to some strange feelings in the mind. This is a spot which bestows a final peace to the mind. Early morning we shall proceed to the spot where Krishna had left his body and then from the bank of Kapila, resume our journey; who knows? we might perhaps get some indication about Krishna...!"

Daaruk agreed with Arjuna's suggestion.

It seemed as if the priest of the Shiva temple had just wound up with final ritual ceremony of the day. The fragrance of flowers and incense was arising out of the door of the Sanctum-sanctorum. After offering worship to Bhagavan Shiva, Arjuna lay down on the mat spread by Daaruk.

"O Daaruk...!" Arjuna spoke after a while and asked, "I am unable to understand one thing. In the Dwarka township, Krishna and Balaram themselves had forbidden consumption of wine. That the Yadavas should not resort to wine, had been Krishna's firm resolve. Then how did all take place here?

Daaruk heaved a deep sigh and looked up at the sky where the constellation of stars were twinkling.

"By merely passing rules, society's welfare cannot be preserved. Krishna had indeed passed Royal orders on the Yadavas to abstain from consuming wine; but the Yadavas had not acknowledged it in the form an in-house discipline. Younger and elder Yadavas, all continued to consume wine stealthily. In spite of the deep respect for Krishna and Balaram, there remained a kind of hostile distance with reference to the question of prohibition, and some difference of opinion had surfaced up. Probably, Krishna thought that instead of binding everyone forcibly to the ruling-discipline…it may to be prudent to provide everyone some kind of freedom to indulge, under the guise of a festival outside the outskirts of Dwaraka… then…then...!…perhaps it may become easier to change everyone to come under the binding of some kind of self-discipline...! Perhaps…!"

Arjuna appreciated the essence of what Daaruk had said. Why the Yadavas alone? even Balaram himself was a lover of wine...! The manner in which Krishna was opposed to wine, was not palatable to the Yadavas. There state was such, that they had to keep up the respect for Krishna, and their liking for wine also!…wine was after all wine…!

"O Kaunteya...!" Daaruk said further, "the time when Saatyaki first and foremost attacked Kritavarma,…at that time, all Yadavas were totally intoxicated with wine. Krishna was the lone sober onlooker—who stood watching everything. After the death of Kritavarma, Saatyaki attacked the Yadavas with the defiled vessels. The very same warriors of the Mahabharata war, who had faced the attacks all the other great warriors; those very warriors were today fighting with each other like cats and dogs, and died biting one another...!"

"And what...? Krishna just stood watching everything, O Daaruk?" Arjuna asked.

"In all probability Krishna must have already foreseen such a miserable plight of the Yadavas, O Dhananjaya...! When all the Yadavas assembled here on this Prabhas-arena…at that time, with some sort of forethought only Krishna did not bring along Uddhava with him. Krishna had told Uddhav, 'O Uddhav...! You now proceed on a pilgrimage...! There is nothing left for you here now...!"

"Krishna was an All-seer...!", said Arjuna softly. He vividly remembered that Vision of his manifestation, on the arena of Kurukshetra...! To the wonder struck Arjuna who had seen the entire universe with the 18 akshauhinis' armies, the sun, the moon, the entire galaxy-space merging into in this Supreme;—Krishna himself had told him, "The destruction of this entire universe is certain, O Paartha...! I am myself its' swallower...! You are a mere instrument...! Even if you don't become the instrument, the destruction of all this is pre-destined...!"

"And in this manner, when even Pradyumna got killed…" Daaruk remembered that dreadful moment—The night had reached its pitch darkness. Far away deep in the forests the cries of jackals could be heard. All of a sudden a shooting star and a glimmering meteor…could be seen piercing through the sky.

"What happened then, Daaruk? Was Krishna watching the scene of Pradyumna being killed by his own kinsmen, in that very same state? Just like a dumb spectator?", Arjuna could not but ask Daaruk.…

"No…! No Dhananjaya…the Krishna who was standing there watching the meaningless destruction with unblinking eyes, suddenly extended his right hand towards the earth and plucked a handful of sharp-pointed grass, the Erak. He then threw that handful of grass on the fighting Yadavas. This handful was transformed into a pestle and started as if raining blows on the fighting Yadavas. This was indeed a sudden attack...! They had lost their poise, and, as such this all destroying attack…and, with the pestle blows the Yadavas were collapsed on to the dust...!" Daaruk thus described he had seen with his own eyes.

That form of Krishna assumed by him when he severed the head of Shishupala with his Sudarshana-chakra, during the Rajasooya Yajna in Indraprastha, appeared in front of Arjuna. And then...! on the ninth day of the Mahabharata, wherein he himself was unable to fight against Gransdsire Bheeshma who was disbanding the entire army….! Even at that time, he had seen a Krishna who had run with his upraised hand wielding the chariot wheel towards Grandsire, he had also seen a Krishna, who created the most powerful conch Paundra out of the bones of that Paundrak who was going about claiming himself to be Vaasudeva, after killing him in single combat—! Arjuna…. Arjuna now stood trembling by the mere imagination of how that Krishna would have appeared, when he was throwing that pointed grass handful at his own lowly behaving kinsmen in a terrifying form personifying his severe destructive mood…!

Perhaps...! perhaps...! as Krishna used to say about himself, that…"this is indeed the destined-path of the embodied Krishna"…that…that-path…! Even that Krishna who had completed the destruction of the Yadavas by throwing a handful of pointed grass at them, perhaps...! even that Krishna may have merged into his own Supreme Form...!"

Arjuna involuntarily closed his eyes…. It was becoming unbearable for him to visualize that scene which was being projected in front of his open eyes...!

When Arjuna's eyes opened, the gentle dawn breeze was fondly waking up nature.

After completing his morning bath and contemplation on spiritual routines, Arjuna performed his morning ritual within the temple compound itself, by putting his offerings into the yajna-kunda. Daaruk lovingly patted the backs of his horses. As soon as the sun's rays stepped out of the sea's skyline and rose above, the chariot set out in search of Krishna along the banks of the Hiran and Kapila rivers.

There was a shoreless expanse on both sides of the foot-pathway. The entire area was idyllic full of natural beauty. Arjuna'a eyes were occupied in absorbing it. Such beauty, that the intoxication of its spreading fragrance was enough to make one inebriated even without wine. Early at dawn, cowherds could be seen taking their cows towards the fields for grazing. In some places groups of maidens going to fetch water were seen. The sound of the chanting and prayers along with some temple's bell was resonating in the atmosphere. Somewhere deep the resonating sound arising out of prayerful chants was whirling around in the air; it was as if the other extreme of creation was striving to unite itself with this end of creation...!

"O Royal son...!" said Daaruk breaking the early morning silence, "There are two paths from here—the right path leads to the confluence of the rivers Hiran and Kapila. It is said that at this confluence, becoming invisible Saraswati is flowing in Pataal. The left path leads to the holy pilgrim-spot of Prachee. When the entire Yadavas were destroyed, at that time, sitting near that holy Pippal tree of Prachee, Krishna had given prayerful offerings."

Arjuna kept staring at that Pippal tree visible from a distance with blank eyes. Once again it flashed before his eyes—that Krishna standing amidst the eighteen Akshauhini-army holding the reins of his chariot—! At that time Krishna had said, "O Arjuna...! among trees I am Ashwattha...!"

And here the Ashwattha itself.

It is somewhere near-about the Ashwattha tree itself, there was a possibility of getting indications about Krishna...!

"Halt the chariot here itself, Daaruk...!" Arjuna gave the orders, "At this confluence of Hiran-Kapila…may be some Ashwattha tree had perhaps spotted Krishna somewhere."

Daaruk pulled the reins, and, the chariot stopped. Arjuna got down.

The full bright daylight had spread all around.

Suddenly, Arjuna's eyes became alert. Bones were lying strewn in some places. Lumps of flesh were lying scattered. His eyes were scrutinizing with speed—seeing the cruel destruction dispersed all around...!

"Daaruk...!" Arjuna's voice choked, and he could not speak.

"Yes, Arjuna...!" replied Daaruk with an emotionless face, "Yes, amidst these, somewhere Saatyaki, Kritavarma, Aniruddha, Pradyumna—all of them must be lying...! Among these itself…somewhere…half eaten flesh by animals, pecked by birds...!—yes...these are the limbs of those very brave heroes, who had given new twist to the history of Aaryavart, O Paartha...!"

Arjuna lowered his eyes. What lay in front of him…he could not bear to see it...! What more could he add to what Daaruk was saying...! Controlling the disgust that arose while crossing over the limbs lying scattered all around… Arjuna somehow proceeded forward.

"Stop...! Stop...!"…from amidst a thick bush that had grown along a corner of the path, hearing a sound suddenly emanating, Arjuna's hands automatically clasped around his Gaandeeva. And then, as if becoming conscious, he withdrew his hands immediately. Daaruk stood staring. Pushing aside the twigs-branches that surrounded the bush, a man came running out and stood in the middle of the path. The hair on his head had grown into dry tresses entwined in such a way that it looked like the nest of a bird. Below the hips was draped with an old-torn-cloth,—all the other limbs were exposed. Eyes were sunk in deep remorse, and over and above, were getting inflated with fear. He appeared as if insane...!

"You? You? You are Arjuna…isn't it?" he said grabbing the chariot.

Arjuna kept staring at him. And then suddenly got down from the chariot…." Yes brother, yes, my name is Arjuna. But…but...! Who are you? And how do you know me? What is your work with me? It looks as if you have been waiting for me here!" It was not clear why Arjuna was asking so many questions. There seemed to be some internal mental disturbance.

That man straightaway fell at the feet of Arjuna, and gradually started as a pitiable groan ended up into a shrill shriek.

"My name is Jaraa (the hunter). I…I…yes I,…O Arjuna, I have killed Krishna…. I have killed Krishna…I have killed Krishna…I have…!"

"What did you say? You…you, Krishna's…the word 'killed' refused to come out of Arjuna's lips…. His lips shrank—yes…reddened...!—His grasp stiffened on the Gaandeeva. It was as if something was boiling within, and he was unable to contain it...! Gripping the dry tressed hair of that man, he hauled him up so ruthlessly....

□

6

Daaruk trembled from head to foot. Arjuna's body started burning like copper. He went on burning. His limbs were trembling as if he were suppressing some internal cyclone. His eyes were spitting fire. Not only the entire Aaryavarta, and not only all the great chariot-warriors,… even his charioteer was familiar with the result of such a state of Arjuna...! Whenever such a state has occurred, there was only destruction...! Daaruk also understood that the tressed hair man's last moments had drawn near, and in this moment of comprehension, a sudden realisation also dawned.

"O great man...!", saying thus he came near Arjuna. He stood so clingingly close to Arjuna, that if he had to even make a small movement, he would have to move Daaruk away…." Forgive me for this indecorum, O Paartha...! But... but...—when this incident about the killing of an unknown helpless and surrendered man…and that too by that son of Paandu, who challenged great warriors like Bheeshma, Acharya Drona, Karna, and even with Shiva himself who is with matted hair by the mere twang of his Gaandeeva...! killed…killed that helpless surrendered man like a mad dog...! then...then...! this incident will put to shame not only those worthy ancestors, but even hundreds of generations to come...!"

"Daaruk...!" said Arjuna, slightly loosening the grip of his strong hands from the head of that tressed man. The released Jaraa once again fell at his feet….This man was saying that he killed Krishna...! Krishna's killing? How is it possible? How could this lowly man do that work, which—Kansa, Jarasandh, Kaalayavan, Paundra, Shishupal—not only that...! even that deadly Kaaliya-serpent and the mighty elephant Kuvalayapeeda could not do?

"Have you forgotten, O Dhananjaya...!" said Daaruk with great caution, glancing at the perhaps down-hearted Arjuna, moving away a little from him, "Sri Krishna himself was a Yadava, and,—mother Gaandhaari had killed that Yadava clan, 36 years in advance itself...!"

Arjuna recollected—In that Vishwaroopa darshan, Krishna himself…must have possibly visualized the emancipation of the embodied Krishna by the hands of this Jaraa. This is after all the line drawn by destiny...! How can this Jaraa kill Krishna? He is a mere instrument...! The destruction of this instrument appointed by destiny—Oh My God...! what a heinous act it would have been, had it happened through his hands...!

"Jaraa...!", Arjuna's voice was now composed...! Arjuna had tightened the reins of restraint over himself...! Placing his hands on his shoulders, he said, "Jaraa...! You are now freed from fear, O friend...! Tell me what is your desire?"

Jaraa lifted up his face and looked at Arjuna. The sparks of anger that were blazing froth from Arjuna's eyes had simmered down. Squatting on the floor itself, he said, "O King...! I am a sinner…! I am a hunter…I used to eke out my living by killing birds and animals…! In the dim light of dawn, seeing Krishna lying under this Pippal tree, I…I…thought that it was…." No sooner had he said this than his voice choked. He lowered his head. Once again he pulled out his voice from within and said, "Thinking that some forest creature was lying there, from far away I shot an arrow."

"Jaraaaa…!" Arjuna's voice came out as a shrill shriek...! It was as if his entire existence was being shaken up. He closed his eyes. His hair got goose-bumps. Once again a wild harshness had surfaced in his voice, "What? Did you shoot at Krishna considering him to be some forest animal? And…and…that arrow of yours stuck Krishna?"

"Yes, O Lord!"…there was no other way left to Jaraa than to meekly acknowledge...! "I shot the arrow, and it went and stuck the sole of Krishna's right heel. That shot arrow…that very moment…that very moment…." Jaraa lost his voice again…. Only a loud cry of anguish escaped from his throat...!

It was as if that moment had got frozen in his eyes...! No word sounds touched the ears of either Jaraa or Arjuna...! Arjuna stood visualising that scene...which shone through the ice-crystals frozen in the eyes of Jaraa…!

Krishna had wanted to sit under the Pippal tree and take rest. Just two quarters of the day earlier, elder brother Balaram had renounced his body in a meditative-state. With elder brother gone, he alone was left as the lone-representative of the Vrishni-clan. All that was dancing before his eyes. As it were, grandsire Vasudeva, and the boy Vajra were left in Dwaraka; but…how many days more would the grandsire also last?

Krishna once more proceeded towards the Prabhas-arena, in order to perform the final rites of elder brother. Night had already crept in. Not only was there darkness on the way, but lying strewn around in the darkness, were the severed limbs of sons, grandsons, great-grand-sons, friends, other venerable elders and kinsmen. Pieces of eaten flesh left behind by wild animals and birds. Krishna continued walking in the midst of the deepening darkness in a totally dispassionate mood. Krishna went on walking over the pathway and along the left-overs of the war-destruction up to the confluence of the rivers Hiran-Kapila, with such natural strides as if nothing but dry-leaves were strewn along the path—a long non-stop journey...! And then the huge Pippal tree could be seen...! Reaching there he stopped. The night is almost on the end. "Why not take little rest? Just until my breathing comes back to normal." Thinking thus he sat down leaning against the tree. His thought was lost in the infinite universe. Contemplating over the Almighty, he closed his eyes.

The moment the eyes closed, Kurukshetra appeared dancing in slow motion in front of him...! In eighteen days, the army of eighteen Akshauhinis had been tuned into ashes. This was the great destructive-war of the Kuru-clan. It was for the sake for the destruction of the wicked ("विनाशाय दुष्कृतां") and for the establishment of righteousness, ("धर्म-संस्थापनार्थाय")...! But now...this gruesome destruction in this holy Prabhas-arena, on the banks of the rivers Hiran Kapila,...why...why has such destruction taken place?!

Krishna slightly opened his eyes and parted his lips into a smile. The Yadava heroes fought each other with weapons. Throwing away the weapons they got into hand to hand scuffle...!

They started throwing empty left-over vessels at each other...! And...then, biting each other like cats and dogs!...and then...then...by the mere touch of the pointed grass, Erak thrown at them by the enraged Krishna, were committed to dust...!

The atmosphere in the very early dawn was full of peace, with cool breeze flowing. In the sky's twilight, foot prints could be seen. Bending his left leg, Krishna placed his right foot over it's knee. Suddenly, Mother Gaandhaari's memory surfaced up...! He closed his eyes. Despite knowing everything, how strange everything seemed to be...!

There was a sort of rustle in the air. An incisive, wettish touch was felt on the sole of Krishna's right foot.

What was it? Krishna opened his eyes—A flow of blood was oozing out of from the sole. A sharp arrow had sunk in the leg.

No...! Krishna did not move even a bit...! He did not even attempt to pull out the arrow. He sat watching the flow of blood, as if from a distance—completely indifferent. And that too just for a short while—Once again he sat gazing at the twinkling stars fading away into the spread out light of the dawn. From somewhere the descent of Supreme power was taking place...!

Dry leaves were heard cackling. Coming out from some distant bushes, a hunter, lying in wait for a prey, had shot an arrow at the tired Krishna. And now...? he was coming running, so that he could recover his prey…and then...? then…he saw—in the blooming twilight of the dawn—! He saw...! "Krishnaaa...!" a scream came out of his throat...!

How could he fail to identify Krishna—with the peacock feather adorning his forehead, his yellow silky dhoti strapped over his waist, and his face shining even in the darkness! And over and above, the fight amongst the Yadavas was still a fresh incident...! Jaraa lost all sense of awareness...! He became extremely uneasy.. "Oh My God...! What have I done?" He just kept on running… "First and foremost, let me remove the arrow which I have shot…!"

Arriving running, he extended his hand to pull out the arrow from the leg. Keenly staring at his restlessness for a moment, Krishna raised his hand in objection….

Jaraa recoiled, and said, "Why? O Lord, Why?"

"Let it be brother...! Do not attempt to make Mother Gaandhaari's words go in vain...!" Krishna replied in a very steady tone.

"I have committed a great sin. Please forgive me, O Lord...! Thinking that you were a jungle animal…I…I… shot an arrow at you. What have I done, O Lord?" saying so, rolling on the ground Jaraa started moaning in a piteous voice.

"Get up, son...!" Krishna said in a compassionate tone, "What is your name?"

"My…my...name is Jaraa...!"

"Jaraa...! OK...!" Krishna let out sweet laughter. Flowing out of the sole, the blood stream had gone a long distance on the ground. "Jaraa...! You name is also significant, son...! Jaraa means old age, never ever leaves anyone...!

Whomsoever the curse of immortality has enveloped,…the great epoch Jaraa swallows him also, isn't it? Jaraa.! you are merely an instrument, son...!"

Did he understand anything? Did he not understand anything? But he kept looking without winking his eyelids. Although he could not have understood Krishna's words spoken in soliloquy, yet they kept ringing in his ears. He himself is but only a hunter—a fowler...!—How can destiny swallow anyone through him?

"State of destiny...! this is indeed the conflict, son...!", said Krishna, "But the only question remaining unanswered, is why the shooting of the arrow was delayed by two quarters of the night?" saying so…Krishna again burst out laughing.

What could poor Jaraa say...! Apart from piteous moaning and wailing, he had nothing left with him.

"Jaraa." After a momentary silence Krishna said. "The body has a limited blood. Its flowing. The supreme being within this body will leave within a moment or two."

"Let me…let me…atone for my action, O Lord...! I cannot live any longer, O Lord, please take me also along with you...!"

"Calm down, brother...!" said Krishna, "there is nothing left for you to do now. Won't you do one work of mine, O friend?"

"Command, O Lord...!"

"Now…my…Krishna's Soul, will return to its original Dham." Krishna said, "Let this earthly body remain in this very state. Arjuna will come here…. You pass on this news to him. And…and…tell Arjuna.." Krishna paused. His eyes started shining. His eyes settled down on his right heel. The blood flowing out from there had slowed down now. Extending his right hand, Krishna touched his right heel. It appeared as if after a Epoch, Gokul stood flashing before his eyes. The onrush of the Kalindi river waters of Vraja Bhoomi became alive…!

The tears from Radha's eyes had dripped exactly at this spot, on the right heel of his leg. At the juncture of his farewell—Placing her head at Krishna's feet, Radha had started sobbing. And then, her tears from her eyes were flowing toward Krishna's heel, in a steady stream...!

After that Krishna never met Radha.

"Jaraa...!" Krishna completed his talk—"Tell Arjuna, to send message to Radha in Gokul, that it is now vain waiting for Krishna. That's all…tell Arjuna to reach the message of Krishna's farewell to Radha in Gokul…. But…not to tell that Krishna had folded up his life making Jaraa's arrow as the instrumental cause...! Let him not tell this news to Radha, that's all, son...! May all end well...!"

"O Bhagavan...O Bhagavan...!" It seemed as if the onrush of the waters of Hiran Kapila rivers started flowing from Jaraa's eyes...! "I have committed a gruesome sin. Bearing the burden of such a great sin I will be unable to live. Please curse me. Please pronounce death-penalty on me. Please push me down into hell. Me…me…into…!"

"May well-being prevail...!" Krishna said once again. His tone was as before steady and calm, but now weaker...! "Sin is not conduct, it is an emotion...! Conduct is merely an instrument, impelled by action—only emotion is soul prompted or soul induced. You are free of emotion, son...! Sin will not touch you…." As he spoke, Krishna closed his eyes. On his lips shone the very same world alluring smile. The hand which rose slightly drooped down. Again a sweet musical-yodel suddenly filled the air. The waters of the Hiran Kapila rivers became still. A unique cool fragrance spread across the atmosphere. There was the touch from invisible soft flowers, in it...!

Breath started flowing in a composed manner within Jaraa who was until now extremely overwhelmed and restless. He realized that he was freed—and burdenless like flowers...! There was not even slightest touch of sin in him. The blood oozing put of Krishna's body was neither red nor black! It was indeed a rainbow, a peacock feather! Amidst the ocean of rainbow and peacock feathers, he heard the flute tune...! And gradually…that intonation set out on an abyssal-infinite journey, and thus slowly started waning…! Jaraa experienced it—he is not hearing the divine tone, he is seeing it...!; not his ears…his eyes were speaking...!

The tone of the flute became motionless. The waters of the rivers Hiran Kapila once again started flowing. Now there remained only the coolness in the air…fragrance remained dissolved.

"Krishna...! Krishna...!" Jaraa let out in shrieks.

And then, just before a moment, that which was known by the name Krishna…in front of that unconscious body, Jaraa stumbled. It was a mere form—The smile on the face was as it is—motionless—but as if drawn on a sketch. A low caste Shudra got the supreme good fortune of witnessing the setting of a great epoch. Surrendering himself to a killer, Krishna folded up his life span. And that folding-up moment dissolved into the universe within the wink of an eye...!

"O King...!", ending his description, crying with spasmodic-outburts, for the first time Jaraa lifted his face and looked at Arjuna. Surmounting the flood of tears, the gaze which reached him, remained as if stunned. Arjuna's face was clouded with an abysmal void, and his eyes were a mere blank, dry, and even desolate...!

The huge Pippal tree was standing just a short distance away from the light of the morning sun's rays...!

"O Parantapa...!" Daaruk said, taking his face near Arjuna's ears, in a loud tone, "Krishna's earthly-body is waiting for Paartha, resting on the Pippal tree.—Until the final-rites are performed, the dharma of the body does not come to an end".

But where was Arjuna?! that he could hear Daaruk's words?!

With a steady-gaze towards the Pippal tree and with unwavering steps, he was going forward slowly, in the same direction, with very slow steps, he finally reached right in front of the lifeless body, the same divine smile on the face, as if consciounsess laden...! The sun's rays were dancing through the leaves of the tree, and twinkling over that smile. Arjuna felt as if Krishna's lips were moving...!

"I am unborn and without beginning seated in the hearts of all. Permeating the earth, I support all beings and send them back to the time-cycle."

Who spoke? Whose words were they?

Amidst the sound of conches and kettle drums—Amidst the dissolution by death—Amidst the great tumult of the eighteen Akshauhini army, thirty-six years back, the words which were uttered by Krishna while he held his chariot's reins,—how could those words be heard here now? Who had repeated them?

With folded hands…Arjuna knelt before Krishna's feet. Calmness had enveloped his restless countenance.

Bending his head he said slowly, "O Achyuta...! You showered such grace, that I may not come under the clutches of delusion once again...! I am Blessed, O Madhusudana...! YOU are indeed, here itself...! here itself...! here…."

□

7

Chariots, horses, bullock-carts and palanquins filled with human beings were silently and slowly moving towards the northern direction. Leaving behind the Raivatak mountain,—Surashtra, Paanchaal, Aanart, and the desert region—each of these regions—after pushing the scenes in their respective regions forward, like a slow motion picture—would slowly recede backwards. In the chariot which was moving in front of the caravan, Arjuna was seated. Many days had passed after leaving Dwaraka, and now the journey through the ever green region of Sapta-Sindhu did not have much distance to be covered. It was only the previous day after taking bath in the Shatadru river, everyone had refreshed themselves out of their tiredness, and now the banks of the holy Bhageerathi, was not very far off.

After performing the last-rites of the five elemental body of Krishna,…Arjuna returned to Dwaraka. The entire Dwaraka-township appeared dreadful like some phantom township. The residents of the town had gathered outside the Fort's-entrance-gate, waiting for Arjuna,…they stood arrayed in groups,…as if everyone was waiting eagerly alert,—so that they may not be labeled as the cause for any delay in leaving for Hastinapur. That jamboree of people in chariots, horses, and bullock carts, appeared like a spread out camp. As soon as Arjuna's chariot entered the base of the Raivatak mountain, many old men and prominent townsmen stepped forward towards Arjuna and told him—

"O best among the Pandavas...! Without any delay—take us away from here. Take us towards some such direction far away from where this Dwaraka devoid of Krishna does not even appear in front of our eyes. Now even looking at this township has become unbearable for us. From the day you left, from that day onwards we stopped entering into the township. We have just been waiting outside this fort waiting for you...."

It was this very fear which had gripped Arjuna also... "How can I set foot into the Krishna devoid Dwaraka? No sooner I see those steeples, my breath may get choked up... beneath which now Krishna is no more there...! Once again today, that very sting was poking from elsewhere.... After performing the final-rites of Krishna's five elemental body with these very hands, how can I return to Dwaraka?"

But Dwaraka supported Arjuna once again. The entire forlorn old men, women...the entire town was standing in front of Arjuna to share his anguish—and,...since the agony was shared, Arjuna also felt a bit consoled. Indeed, Krishna had told the truth, "I am 'unmodified-personification'. I am pervading in each and every creature, Gudaakesh...!" Horses, cows, bullocks, all in their silent speech were telling, "We shall not set foot on Dwaraka, O Dhananjaya...! Come, take us to Hastinapur." Along with all kinsmen, Rukimini, Satyabhama, and all other women of Dwaraka drowned in grief—were waiting for Arjuna. All the gates of the fort were open. Filling-up the moats around the fort, the waters of the sea were lashing against the supportless, unguarded open gates, and trying to push forward onto the paths.

Arjuna looked toward the sea. In the normally aimless lashing waves, today some special meaning could be visualized—Now that Krishna was not there, it seemed as if everyone had abandoned their decorum...! That is why it appeared as if the waters of the seas which would normally wash the feet of Dwaraka during Krishna's presence today, in the absence of Krishna was attacking the mansions of

Dwaraka! Arjuna kept looking at these decorumless waves for a few moments, and then turned his back, and marched towards the northern direction.

Legs were moving, wheels of the vehicles were rolling. The neighing of the horses and the rumbling sounds of the chariots! Indeed! these were the only proof left of any sign of Nature's sentience; the rest seemed as if they had immersed their entire consciousness in the moats of Dwaraka... and a mere mass of humans was now moving forward...! Normally, no one can take their eyes off the alluring beauty of the Sapta-Sindhu region. But today, everyone's eyes were stuck on the western horizon, as they walked on the path passing through the middle of the Shatadru and Dvashadvati rivers...! And now...Bhageerathi was not far off...! And indeed across the Bhageerathi, there was hardly any distance to Hastinapur...! The time for setting foot over the Hastinapur's soil was drawing near...!

"Kaunteya...!" Suddenly, the nostrils of horses of the foremost chariots started swelling up, and they pulled back both front legs on to the earth. The chariot stopped. Daaruk pulled the reins. His voice was trembling, "The horses are refusing to move forward...!"

Arjuna became absolutely alert. His hand reached out over the Gaandeeva. He looked around in all directions. The chariot stopped. The entire train of chariots, and horses behind, suddenly stopped! The armed travellers walking alongside on both sides of the path also became alert, seeing the frown on Arjuna's face.

On the western direction, there was a high ramp. From there, suddenly a loud commotion was seen. Even as one was looking,—out from behind the towering rocks, all at once, a group of countless armed men came and stood onto the middle of the road. Some armed men came and stood high above on both sides of the path.

"I, Kurkat, the Aabhir Commander, command all of you to hand over all your wealth, young maidens, and well-bred horses to our warriors. If you delay even for a moment you stand to lose your lives...!" A sturdy, strong man standing in front sounded the fearsome-twang of his bow string, announcing their intentions.

"Kurkat...!" Arjuna trembled with rage, "Know that your death, and that of your army is near at hand...! The piercing arrows of the ambi dexterous Arjuna, victor of the Mahabharat war, will instantaneously transport you and your friends to region of death."

"Arjuna...?" Kurkat said mockingly, "Indeed...! Yes...I too had heard that a great battle had taken place a few years back. But,...do you know? in that war there were no Aabhirs; there was no Kurkat...! Good...! at least I am seeing one of the vestiges of that war...!"

How could Arjuna bear this? Quickly, he lifted his Gaandeev, and placed his hand on the bow string. But by now the soldiers of Kurkat, considering Arjuna's presence to be as insignificant as grass, pounced upon the Yadava soldiers. They disbanded the entire Yadava chariots, horses, bullock carts,—in a matter of moments...!

"Daaaaruk...!" Arjuna shrieked out, "Daaruk, Why has the Gaandeev become so heavy today? And…the arrows in my sheath…?"

Arjuna could shoot some arrows with great difficulty, and all of them scattered hither-thither in the air, like the arrows shot by some novice archer. Arjuna's body became weak and recognizing the situation...Kurkat moved forward and caught hold of the ears of the horses of Arjuna's chariot.

"Arjuna...! This is not Kurukshetra...! What is this pitiable state of yours'? The One,...who bragged of having won the war of Mahabharat by the mere twang of his bow? What a pitiable state is this? Look Arjuna, just cast your glance in that direction…." Kurkat drew Arjuna's attention to the scene.

Arjuna once again composed himself, alerted himself; but the Gaandeev refused to remain steady in his hands.

In the same exasperation, he shot some arrows at Kurkat. But not one of them reached its target. The shrieks of the Yadava women were becoming louder. Without any resistance, the Yadava soldiers had surrendered, and Arjuna having forgotten all knowledge of his archery, was standing helpless.

Kurkat once again mocked at him.

Arjuna cast his glance over the helpless Yadava-commune. Kurkat's soldiers had taken in their hands,… custody of all horses, wealth, etc.

"Daaruk, Daaruk...!" Arjuna roared. He lifted the Gaandeev with both his hands in order to shoot at Kurkat's forehead. But let alone the arrow shooting forward...! the Gaandeev slipped out of his hands and fell on the chariot. And with its jerk, Arjuna himself staggered. It had never happened like this before…! Arjuna and without his Gaandeev? What was all this happening? This was the same Gaandeev, which at his mere hint would become light as a flower, and, he would wield it as he wished, and twang it...! But…but…today…?

"Dhananjay...!" Daaruk cautioned Arjuna, "O Revered one, this dilemma is in vain...! Just cast your glance there—Seeing you, the ambidexterous one, the Gaandeev-bearer Arjuna, defeated,...! the Yadava women are welcoming the victory of the enemy…."

"Meaning?" Arjuna turned and looked back, and was stunned. That inner helplessness by which he was distressed!—the piteous scene which he saw in front of him was many a time more distressing;…—by their own sweet will,…the Yadava-women were going along with Kurkat's cowherds...!

"You have seen with your own eyes, Arjuna..." punching on the backs of the horses of the chariot, Kurkat said, "these are women, who always choose only victory...! The barrenness of your arrows has revealed to them your helplessness...! See O Arjuna, women and wealth have been created only for the victors; defeated and cowardly men cannot protect them. That is why these women themselves have conceded to become the wedding-garlands of the victors...!"

"Lowly among men, Kurkat...! Shut up...!" Arjuna made a last effort, "The women whom you are insulting… those women belong to Yadunandan Krishna and Plough-bearer Balaram."

Even before he could complete the sentence, Kurkat blew his conch. The sound of the conch resounded in all directions.

"Devi Satyabhama...!" saying so Arjuna jumped out of the chariot and started running. But his legs staggered and even as he tried to balance himself,…he stumbled on to the ground.

"Don't be afraid, Arjuna...!" Kurkat said sarcastically, "My soldiers will not even touch these old women. Your entire army has become mine…. Our goal is fulfilled, except young maidens and wealth, nothing else is of use to me. The wealth I have won, and the women are out of their sweet-will competing to win the favour of the victors.—you yourself are witnessing it...!"

Kurkat's words were bitter, his words were harsh; but what was the truth behind them? And after all,...it cannot be denied...! The young Yadava maidens were themselves holding the hands of the cowherd soldiers, and going with them, out of their own sweet-will, laughingly.

"Daaruk..."Arjuna said keeping his eyes open with great difficulty, "These noble women of the Krishna Balaram lineage…."

"Now Krishna and Balaram are no more there, O Kaunteya...!" Daaruk said despondently.

After some time Arjuna opened his eyes. Kurkat and his soldiers were climbing up the ramp. The Yadava commune was completely shattered. Most of the soldiers were killed at the hands of the cowherds, some were lying half-dead.

"Daaruk...!" Arjuna said slowly, "Who had won the Mahabharat war?!"

His sad eyes looked down steadily at the Gaandeev.

Daaruk remained silent. His eyes welling up with tears were speaking volumes for his feelings. Just as he had experienced shock on seeing Krishna's earthly body, today he felt more stunned at this mystery....

A terrible roar arose, pounded upon Arjuna's ears, and alerted him.

"...O Parantapa! This Bheeshma, this Drona, this Jayadratha, and this Karna—I have killed everyone of them. They are dead. Without grieving, you become a mere instrument in killing them, O Paartha...." Who had said this? When? To whom? It was as if a curtain had dropped of from his eyes...!

It was Krishna who had made him victorious in the Mahabharata war. Now Krishna is no more. The victor of Mahabharat, Arjuna, was a mere instrument. Bheeshma, Drona, Jayadratha, and Karna—Who had killed all these people? What a misconception it was?

"Daaruk...!" Arjuna said very slowly, "Are you seeing the power of the Krishna devoid Arjuna? Just consider this as a body devoid of its life force...! It is strange, O Brother, that despite knowing this, one does not understand it...!"

"What does one not understand, O Paartha!"

"How did the Yadava women, by their own sweet-will go after these uncultured, wild cowherds...?"

"O Dhananjaya!" Daaruk said, "Those whom we cannot protect, for them it is indeed Nature's Law to seek safety elsewhere.... Kurkat was the victor...and the fact that women should always make their own arrangements for their personal safety, by putting the wedding garland on the victor.... This...this...is but natural, O Dhananjaya!"

Arjuna became calm and composed.

With the help of the remaining soldiers and others, having repaired the battered vehicles, and making them serviceable, Arjuna once again set out on the journey. Hardly half of the commune was remaining…. As it is, the conscious force had left.... Now what was left? It looked as though countless ants were dragging a dead snake…. Alas, only that hearts' palpitations were left. Where they were all going? It was as if no one knew anything about it themselves….

The sun had started setting. The afternoon journey was passing along continuously, as if an aim-less journey…. It is only when the legs of the dumb cows started faltering, then only there seemed to be signs of life….

From a distance, the banks of Bhageerathi could be seen. Over her frosty waters, the sun's rays could be seen shining over her ripples, as if spreading golden nets over her. And, even beyond this net, a man, lit-up and draped by a golden light, could be seen, offering oblations, and performing his evening-rites.

"O great warrior!" Daaruk called out.

"No Daaruk, no...!, now this salutation is meaningless. You have seen with your own eyes Arjuna's wretched plight, isn't it?" Arjuna said despondently.

Daaruk remained silent, and then went on to ask, "Shall we plan to camp here for the night?"

Arjuna got down from the chariot. Daaruk started making arrangements. When his eyes fell upon the motions of a sage performing evening rites on the banks of Ganges, his eyes started opened wide in wonder…. After completing his mantra-chantings, the sage came near Arjuna—

"O Son of Pritha...!" coming very close to Arjuna, he involuntarily called out to Arjuna.

Arjuna was flabbergasted...!

"Uddhav...! You? You...here?" It was as if, wonder had assumed a form, and sprung out of his mouth in the form of words….

"Yes, Arjuna", said Uddhav, "Krishna had sent me on a pilgrimage. Any news of Dwaraka?" And at that time his eyes fell on groups of people setting up camps here and there, on the open ground. Suddenly, his tone changed. And his face showed anxiety. He asked, "What is this I am seeing, O Paartha? These townsmen from Dwaraka?"

"Uddhav?" said Arjuna slowly, "Dwaraka is no more there—Now Dwaraka is nowhere at all, O Uddhav! Now we shall not be able to see Dwaraka anywhere, at any time...."

Uddhav closed his eyes. His lips moved as if murmuring. As if saluting Nature, he folded his hands in such a way, and, bent his head.

"Not only Dwaraka, the entire Dwaapar Epoch has folded into the infinite time, O Arjuna...!" said Uddhav, "As if the eternal Sun has set...!"

The blanket of the dark night, folded up the Sapta-Sindhu completely.

□

8

Without getting the least perturbed, Uddhav listened to this heart rending story from Arjuna's mouth, with full attention. It was already late in the night. Tired lost, the defeated Yadavas were lying hither-thither on the banks of Bhageerathi, as if they had become an integral potion of that darkness. Even the remaining horses and bullocks were taking rest in that same darkness. Arjuna finished his narration, and once again turned towards the flow of Ganges in front of him. The flow appeared as if she had not heard even a word of Arjuna—she kept flowing,…that's all...! Arjuna looked toward Uddhav. In the dim light of the moon—even the face of Uddhav appeared like the flow of Ganges….

"Uddhav...?" becoming perplexed Arjuna said, "even after listening to this awesome story, nothing is happening to you?"

Uddhav laughed.

Arjuna became still more perplexed...!

"You…you…are laughing Uddhav? What has happened to you?"

"Nothing has happened to me, Arjuna". Uddhav broke his long silence, saying, "Brother, through my eyes, only the flow of Ganges can be seen. Krishna's eyes could fathom both the beginning and end of the Ganges clearly"….

"End of the Ganges?"

"Yes, O son of Pritha...!" Even this Ganges was not there one day. In order to liberate the sons of Sagar, Bhageerath brought her from Heaven; if tomorrow another Bhageerath of Heaven takes her back, then what is the wonder in it, O revered one! This Sapta-Sindhu, this Bhageerathi, this Himalayas—all of them, sometime or other will certainly dissolve into the fold of destiny. Perhaps this may occur thousands of years hence—but,... who are we to measure time? Where and when could we measure the expanse of Himalayas or her outpouring? In the same way, destiny…."

"Uddhav!"

"Yes, revered one!" Uddhav's eyed turned towards the sky, "When the Yadavas left on the journey to the Prabhas-arena—the previous evening whatever Krishna had told me…. I had not understood even the hint behind it...—Today, I realized…"

"What had Krishna said, Uddhav?" there was eagerness in Arjuna's voice.

"Krishna had indeed said…." Uddhav's eyes stopped blinking…. "Uddhav...! Brother, yesterday night in my sleep state, I felt the experience of rat-bite…." Calling Uddhav near, Krishna was telling him in such a low tone, as if whispering in his ears.

"What is this you are telling, O Madhusoodan?" Hearing the words of Krishna, Uddhav had become restless, "Even in a sleep-state, for a trivial creature like a rat to bite you?"

"In the kingdom of eternal time cycle there is no trivial creature, Uddhav...! It and only it is powerful—all the rest of existence are mere instruments...!" Krishna had become serious…. And said, "Have you forgotten, Brother,…the term of Mother Gaandhaari's curse is coming close to its end…36 years after the great battle, the Vrishni-clan….

Krishna left the sentence unfinished; but, Uddhav understood it fully. He could merely utter only one word, "Krishna...!"

"Rat-bite...! This is the hint from destiny...!" Krishna said,

"Accepting this hint, whosoever sits at the feet of destiny, it does not touch him…! One who does not recognize it, destiny dissolves such a stupid one within the horizon of the universe; and,…for him, who even after understanding, does not accept it, time eternal does not allow such a fool to remain anywhere, either in the world or in the extra terrestrial worlds…."

Uddhav wished that Krishna keeps on talking; if he keeps on talking how nice it would be...!

"The Yadavas are wine lovers, Uddhav...! Even for Balaram himself this ban on wine is becoming undesirable. Everyone, all around are hiding and drinking quietly like thieves. I know all this. The moment the Yadavas come to know that I know all about this teachery and am still not doing anything about it, that very moment all decorum will vanish and after that…these Yadavas will start drinking in front of Krishna; and then, I cannot ignore it, Uddhav…that will become unbearable for me!"

"Why don't you stop them, O Vaasudeva?" asked Uddhav in a childlike simplicity.

"Now any attempt to stop them is in vain, Uddhav…" said Krishna, "Such stopping would amount to violation of destiny's hint"…!

Then after stopping for a while, Krishna said, "Along with all these Yadavas and elder brother Balaram, we shall go to the Prabhas-arena. Prohibition is in Dwaraka, not in Prabhas-arena...."

"Meaning…?"

"Did not understand, Uddhav?" said Krishna's with his alluring smile widening, "All restrained activities here will become unrestrained there. And there its decorumless face will reveal itself. All discriminative faculty will be lost…and only this loss of discrimination, will make mother Gaandhari's words fructify...!"

"O Krishna...Krishna...! Knowing about this devastation also?"

"Yes, knowing it also…! Knowing it also, I can't stop it…this indeed, is the greatness of destiny?" Again the same alluring smile of Krishna...! "Uddhav...! Time eternal touches only those whose work is completed...! Krishna Balarama and all the Yadavas' pre-destined deeds, have now come to an end…but…. Uddhav, for you, just for you only...one work is left to be done…."

Uddhav stood dazed….

Even after the deeds of the entire Vrishni clan have been completed, what deed can indeed be left for Uddhav to do? He started searching for an answer on Krishna's face.

"That work you will come to know at the appropriate time." Suddenly, Krishna's tone underwent a change; it was as if some command was being given from far away, "Tomorrow morning you start off on a pilgrimage, Brother. The future of the Prabhas-arena is not for you…."

"O Vaasudev…O Govind...!" said Uddhav in an overwhelming tone—"How will I be able to see you on the pilgrimage journey?"

"O revered one...!" said Krishna, "Soul does not disappear by the good and bad of the body. From now on you have darshan of that Soul in the sky".

Uddhav had no reply, hence remained silent...!

"Ohh...! Perhaps this is that remaining work…!" Uddhav could not utter whatever words he wanted to say. Indeed…hearing about that particular evening from Uddhav...it was certain that Arjuna had started seeing that scene of Dwaraka clearly...! A glimmer came about in his eyes. He blurted out, "Go to Gokul, O Uddhav...! Krishna's message has to be conveyed to Radha...."

Arjuna had not forgotten Jara's words; listening to Uddhav's narration, those words came alive again. Perhaps it was because of this work only, Krishna had bailed Uddhav out of the Yadava clan. Who else but Uddhav can be a more worthy person, in order to deliver this heavy message to Radha?

"Radha..." Arjuna uttered the word, but within some kind of tingling arose...!

Arjuna saw that—Uddhav also was slightly disturbed.

Now in front of Uddhav, there was no Bhaageerathi waters. Krishna, Dwaraka, or Arjuna also were not there. In front of his eyes, there was the gurgling and dancing Kalindi river…that Kadamba tree…and the Govardhan mountain...! The cows and the Gopis playing the Raas-leela; And…that one Gopa-kanya?

How can I tell Radha that now, both, the water of Kaalindi and the Kadmaba tree…. Both have become devoid of consciousness?

"And, Uddhav! Krishna has also said this…" Arjuna completed the message…. "The manner in which Krishna's body got dissolved…do not describe anything about that, to Radha. Just say…Krishna's body has dissolved…. That's all…nothing more should be said…."

Uddhav remembered everything…like a lightning—When Kansa had sent for Krishna to come to Mathura, at that time, the Krishna who left Gokul and went with Akroor…could never ever return to Gokul. Mathura, Dwaraka, Indraprasth, Hastinapur, Praagjyotishpur—and to many other places Krishna had kept on going and coming.... Alas! It was only the Vrajabhoomi which always remained deprived of him….

Radha….

Perhaps this young daughter of Vrajabhoomi may be waiting for Krishna even now...! In order to welcome her Shyam, she may be sitting with unblinking one pointed eyes, looking in the direction of Mathura.

"Your unblinking eyes shall remain ever hanging thus, O Radha", murmured Uddhav—But immediately he pulled back his lips to close very tightly.—Why? Why was it? That Krishna wished that Radha should not be informed about the full story of the dissolution of his body? And? And…? Why did such a mundane human eagerness surface up...?

Even in such a distinguished personality like Krishna, for wanting to pass on this message to Radha! And then?" Uddhav suddenly got up with a start...!

It was as if he became conscious on the issue of Krishna. What is all this I am thinking? How can there be such a question about Krishna? And, thinking thus, he felt a bit ashamed also. Has anyone ever understood anything about Krishna completely? Perhaps only Radha can unravel my quandary.

"OK...! I shall become the instrument to fulfill this last work of Krishna..." said Uddhav, "I shall go to Gokul. I shall tell each and every sand particle of Vrajabhoomi—that....Now Krishna's being has become pervasive in all these sand particles!" And then his tone changed. Suddenly, Uddhav's ears stood up stiff, "Dhananjaya...! Did you hear some sound swimming over the flowing onrush of Ganges?"

Arjuna became alert. Apart from the gurgling sound of the onrush, everything else was soundless. But…there was something, which only Uddhav was able to hear.

"Even if fire is not manifested, its existence does not get destroyed, Uddhav! The main reason for sorrow is attachment…."

Krishna himself had told him about this while starting off on the pilgrimage. These very words of Krishna, he will tell each and every sand particle of Vrajabhoomi. How simple is this thought….

"Arjuna...!" By the mere feel of those words, Uddhav's voice changed. The moment of distress had been overcome, "Early morning tomorrow, our paths will become separate. Before we become subservient to our duties, I have to tell you something...."

Arjuna was listening to Uddhav's words.

"After being defeated at the hands of a lowly and beastly cowherd army commander…" Uddhav's voice got stuck up.

"Carry on, Uddhav, tell me without any hesitation. I am still not able to comprehend this defeat...."

"That is why I am telling you, O Paartha...! The scene which you saw during those moments of defeat—The Yadava women out of their own sweet will, rejected your protection; in front of Kurkat, you and your Gaandeev were proved to be pygmies—All this...as expressed by Krishna, was the hint of destiny, O Arjuna! Now realising this indication..." again Uddhav got stuck up.

"What Uddhav? what now? Uddhav?"

"Now surrendering the remaining years of the life journey to the Almighty, one should merely execute his outward duties with this body, O Arjuna! More than this, perhaps, only Yudhishthir will be able to explain you...." Uddhav moved away his eyes and finished what he had to say. He closed his eyes. He did not even know when sleep occupied his eyes...!

However, there was no sign of sleep in Uddhav's eyes.

With the help of his memory cords, that form of the boy Krishna which Uddhav would remember it was that very form that had kept him bound. Defeat of Kaaliya, killing of Dhenukaasur, Bakaasur, the Govardhan bearing Krishna.... When all these incidents took place, Uddhav was with Krishna. Uddhav was not unfamiliar with any aspect of Krishna. In the end when he left off on the pilgrimage, even at that time, Krishna had opened out his knowledge casket in front of him, and indeed...whatever golden words...he had uttered....

Even then what did Uddhav know anything about Krishna at all? During the last moments of folding up his life-span, Krishna remembered Radha—that Radha, whom Krishna never met after leaving Gokul...that Radha, about whom Krishna never ever mentioned in front of anyone... that Radha, who had occupied Krishna's heart to such an extent...today...today...Uddhav was getting goose-bumps, knowing all this.... He had become absorbed, on this form of Krishna....

Krishna was super human, a great human thought Uddhav may be.... But...at this juncture, this human form of Krishna...this was appearing extremely exhilarating... chanting the name of Krishna.... Radha, the other women falk of Vraj—Uddhav had seen all of them. But while chanting Radhaa's name...to get Krishna's look! This good fortune only that hunter Jaraa had got, isn't it? Such a pang arose in Uddhav's mind. Great respect towards Jaraa did arise in Uddhav's mind...that final moment...in which whatever last scene must have emanated in that presence of Krishna.... In that...only Radha might have been there? Or, may be the entire Vrajabhoomi might have been there? And if at all it had been the entire Vrajabhoomi, then in that scene, certainly he himself was sure to have been there, somewhere or other. Whilst folding up his life-span with this recollection of yester-years, how refulgent Krishna's face might have appeared? And...indeed...a sight worth seeing.... In such imagination.... Uddhav's mind got lost somewhere....

He raised his eyes towards the East. The sun's rays were about to surface up. There was not yet any sign of any movement in the tired-sleeping Yadava travellers. Arjuna was lying sense-less next to Uddhav. Uddhav remained looking at his face. Pity for Arjuna arose in his mind. Hope it was not effect of the topic about the indications of destiny, which he had told Arjuna just some time back?

A thought line was once been drawn in Uddhav's mind. After completing the final duty of conveying the message to Radha, perhaps! even after that...there might be some indication about the future. Just as Krishna was saying, "I too, have surrendered myself at the feet of time eternal." This indication is for everyone!

Indeed...! just as the decision became resolute, all obstacles dropped off.

Taking up the Kamandalu (a water pot used by the ascetic) in his hands, Uddhav arose and stood up. Casting a glance at the onrush of Ganges waters, he contemplated the Almighty and then proceeded to perform the morning rituals.

When Arjuna opened his eyes, at that time, Uddhav was standing in waist high waters of the flow of Ganges, and was saluting the dawning sun's rays.

□

9

On the royal roads of the majestic palatial mansions in Hastinapur, glowing under Maharaja Yudhishthir's glorious rule, the sun's rays once again shone—and the whiteness of the mansions which were being lit up, appeared now like faint shadows—And, on the royal road there was a chariot—it was that of Arjuna.

The eyes of the kinsmen eagerly waiting to see the Gaandeev bearing Arjuna, automatically turned downwards seeing the Gaandeev devoid Arjuna today.... The scars of Gaandeev on the shoulders, and the marks of the quiver also were clearly visible. But? This way.... An unarmed Arjuna? Such a form of Arjuna had never been seen by the kinsmen. Lowering their weapons, the sentries of the Royal Palace, appropriately welcomed Arjuna—it was difficult to infer whether Arjuna had seen them or not... and, it was not possible also to infer. He was coming out after visiting his mansion. He had left back his Gaandeev and all other Royal regalia, and had come to offer his bows to Maharaja Yudhishthir.

As for the Royal splendors, everything was as they had been—in their respective places, as desired.... The flags fluttering over the domes and the festoons tied over the windows bore ample proof of the welfare of the kingdom. There was movement among the horses, and the stable boys were busy in their own works. All the other servitors also were busy with their respective jobs. All eyes went up involuntarily, and paused in a stare at Arjuna for a moment. Arjuna felt as if he could not bear these stares.

Taking long steps, Arjuna started going towards the rest-room of elder brother. Yudhishthir was right in front—as if he was standing there expecting him. Seeing him thus suddenly in front, Arjuna was taken a back a little; and then he remembered—Daaruk had come bringing the message of Krishna, and he had also left from Hastinapur along with him only. On that day, Maharaj Yudhishthir had placed his hands on his head and blessed him, "Dhananjay! O brother! Krishna is indeed looking after the welfare tasks for Dwaraka and the Yadavas; but, return soon, bringing news about his well-being, and bring all news about Madhav. We shall all be waiting for you."

Indeed, Arjuna did return—returned to Hastinapur itself—and the waiting of Maharaj Yudhishthir also came to an end, but,...the well-being of whom Maharaj was expecting to know....his well-being? What will Arjuna tell him,...that Krishna?

But, no...! He will not have to take up the difficult responsibility of conveying this tough and inauspicious news to Yudhishthir. Because, even on the main royal-roads of Hastinapur, indications had started appearing, and it meant, that, that news has already spread here like some dark clouds.

The Gaandeevless body of Arjuna...and over and above, mere tell tale marks of the existence of Gaandeev were seen, but, with Gaandeev missing.... Were these not enough to speak volumes about some foreboding?

Arjuna moved forward and prostrated at elder brother's feet. "O elder Brother!" His eyes bent down, and his head too.

"May all be well, revered one..." said Yudhishthir placing his hands on younger brother's head.

"I have lost the right to well-being, Maharaj..." said Arjuna.

"Calm down, brother! I have already got the news. I heard all about Krishna's great departure also, and also of your defeat at the hands of the cowherds...."

Arjuna somehow kept composing himself. And then said, "That Krishna, who always protected us in the Mahabharat war,.... In the absence of that Krishna, I could not carry out even one task entrusted to me by him...! 'Such unfitness, such incapacity?' I was unsuccessful in protecting the Yadava women,...how can I forget its sting?" with great discomfort Arjuna fumble with those words.

Yudhishthir held Arjuna's hands like a small child's, and took him along with him with great concern, and made him sit in the seat next to himself, and then placing his hands on his head said, "Revered one, the sting about which you are talking, that sting certainly has some meaning behind it...! O Arjuna...! If at all we consider Krishna's departure as a part of a controversial natural sequence, then is not your defeat at the hands of the cowherds also a part of that sequence? This...this defeat...is not an indication of your—our failure...." Pausing for a moment, Yudhishthir cast his glance at Arjuna's face. As if wishing to see him freed from pain, he once again said, "This is a message indicating the end of our life's-purpose, O revered one...!"

Arjuna was left speechless.

"O elder brother!" Arjuna suddenly remembered Uddhav's words.

"Yes, revered one, do you know? that nowadays...in the dishes being served in golden vessels, I feel as if vermins are crawling!" Yudhishthir closed his eyes..."At midnight, bleating of goats and howling sounds of jackals resound in the ears, and sleep gets disturbed."

"O Maharaj...all these indications...!"

"Yes Arjuna, all these are indications, which are telling us that after the completion of life's purpose, one should recognize the path ordained to be followed. After the completion of Krishna's body's final rites, the time for our last journey has also come near. Even before death takes us in his hideous jaws, we should accept the life's ordained natural course...!"

Without giving Yudhishthir a chance to stop, Arjuna said,—"How is it to be done, elder brother? What is the meaning of accepting the ordained natural course? Committing suicide is not permitted by the scriptures, isn't it? That is the path of despair and failure…."

"Yes, suicide is not accepted by the scriptures, but, there is a way out, Arjuna...! Without forcibly putting an end to the body, if we accept the great departure, then that does not amount to suicide, son! That is merely to accept the course of time humbly..." said Yudhishthir, "The direction in which father Dhritarashtra, mother Gaandhaari and Kunti went—O Arjuna, the direction in which uncle Vidur went…the voice is being heard from that direction. O Brother, I cannot ignore that voice now. It is indeed good that whilst returning from Dwaraka, you too heard this voice. Make preparations for coronating Parikshit…."

"Elder Brother! Arjuna suddenly asked in such a way, as if wanting to know some secret. "Will we find Krishna in that direction?"

"Perhaps we may find him…! There could be some message also from Krishna near the valleys of mountains of Himaadri, Brother! But understand this much, that after this, our remaining duty would be to attain Krishna only…. Come get up son!" Yudhishthir placed his hands on Arjuna's shoulder, "Till today it has always been that Krishna searched us out and helped us. Today that work we have to do…come on, let us all surrender unto Nature, and go in search of Krishna…."

Yudhishthir got up.

What Krishna had told him; that which Uddhav had told Arjuna; and now, that which Yudhishthir is telling—everything became a puzzle…Arjuna began trying to connect up the chain formed by the links of these three utterances in his mind. That which Uddhav saw through Krishna's eyes…may be Yudhishthir also saw the same thing. O Krishna...! To how many people you bestowed eyes!

Once again Arjuna mentally reached the fields of Kurukshetra. He could never forget those moments.... When he was sitting soaked in sweat, fatigued, helpless in the chariot...at that time that which Achyuta had told him....

And that...which the victor Arjuna of the Mahabharat battle...had once again told Krishna in the mansion of Hastinapur....

"O Ghanshyam! That which you had told me in Kurukshetra, is again and again coming back in my mind. I wish to once again hear all those words from you...."

Krishna's laughter rippled out...! Indeed, the same ever fresh Krishna's laughter...." You are searching for the Krishna of Kurukshetra in Hastinapur, O Revered one? How is it possible?"

"At that moment my mind was filled with despondency, O Mohan...!" said Arjuna, "My mind had wavered in a dilemma. In that moment of dilemma, no doubt I heard many things, but somethings are being forgotten also...I wish to hear all that once again, Keshav!"

As if addressing some person standing faraway, "Just as the Arjuna of Kurukshetra is different from today's Arjuna, so too, today's Krishna also is different from that Krishna who had manifested at that moment, O Gudaakesha!" He was talking as if not about himself, but about someone else; he was talking with so much detachment, "Perhaps this is the only opportunity for an embodied one to comprehend this truth. The embodied one is not someone who is self-created, Arjuna, he is a mere instrument. The truth manifested by an embodied one is merely the truth of that moment. One who misses the chance in attaining the truth of that moment...for him! a new truth gets manifested. This is the mechanics of truth which is eternal O son!"

"Give me knowledge of that eternal truth, Achyuta!" Arjuna prayed to Krishna.

But now whatever Krishna told him, everything was in it but…that twang of Kurukshetra was missing…. There was no darshan of the divine manifestation in it, the resounding of the Paanchajanya was missing—The presence of the Sudarshan-chakra also was not there….

This is exactly what Krishna had also said—

"The embodied one is not self-created, Arjuna! He is a mere instrument…."And…and Krishna himself? He also was after all an embodied one!

It flashed in Arjuna's mind—Those duties, those decorums of the embodiment from which Krishna himself was not free…How? how can Arjuna and the Pandavas be free from them? When Krishna himself was not able to repeat the Gita's knowledge, then how can the Gaandeev wielding Arjuna of Kurukshetra, again and again repeat that capability? How childish this very wish was? And when the mind had reached this argument, then, suddenly Arjuna became devoid of mental-burden—and felt very light…. He took a long breath, and then he realized that he was left alone in the room…. Yudhishthir had left long back…. He got up and walked towards Draupadi's residence.

The news of Arjuna's arrival had already reached Draupadi. She was standing at the door itself. As soon as she saw Arjuna, her face brightened, and that shine was not an ordinary shine…it was saying. "Even amidst the smoke rings of the extinguished yajna-fires, make me feel the Light of your existence" such was that shine. With unblinking eyes she kept seeing Arjuna.

"Yaajnasenee! coming near Arjuna gently called out.

As if she had not heard anything, Draupadi stood there motionless! Her face was completely devoid of emotions and it was as if the twinkle in her eyes were also…as if roaming somewhere—

"Krishnaaaa...!" Arjuna placed his hand gently upon her shoulder.

"Paaarth...!" Draupadi's lips did indeed flutter, but, after these two words, they could not remain open.... Her voice became strangulated, and the Kalindi river like tears welled up in her eyes—as if there was some blockage inside, that had suddenly slipped out....

Arjuna remained stunned!

"What is this Draupadi? Those eyes in which there were no tears even when Dushasan had disrobed you and...from which fire had been raining...during the days when we were dweling in forest, Jayadratha had attempted to kidnap you, then too you had not cried—And, indeed... when Keechak had done such great insult in Virat Nagar, then also the eyes in which there were no tears...only fire had manifested.... Why has that fire from those eyes extinguished in this manner, today?"

As if searching in her memory matrix for a reply, fumbling thus for words, she said, "Yes, O Ambidextrous one, yes.... During each and every moment of those incidents, Krishna was present indirectly everywhere... have you forgotten that? During the wicked disrobing incident...what could not be accomplished by five husbands and Grandsire himself—That Krishna had done! In the midst of the sorrows of the forest life, in order to save us from the anger fire of Durvaasa...that was indeed Krishna only! He was the one who had eaten the left-over grain of food from the Akshayapatra...and? and? Now? now? That involvement is not there, that basic breath of life itself is not there...". Drowning herself in the past and heart broken, Draupadi began wailing bitterly.

Arjuna could not utter a word. That moment of the disrobing scene began dancing in front of him. But now, in these moments of recollection, there was profound pity in his eyes; there was no sign of any passion or shock showing up. Those days in Virat Nagar flashed back in the mind; that day came back in the memory; that Krishna came back in the memory.... That Krishna...in order to save us from the wrathful Rishi Durvaasa's curse... had eaten a grain like left-over food from Draupadi's Akshayapatra—! That Krishna has now dissolved, unto Infinity....

"Krishnaa!" said Arjuna, "do you know, this dissolution of his influence has a deeper indication? It is the indication that our life's purpose had come to an end, Draupadi. Now there is no past, no future, neither any present—In order to attain that supreme moment wherein all these three tenses may become one,...we have to prepare for the great exit.... Perhaps, that influence of Krishna which we have lost, we may get somewhere in the snow-peaked mountains of Himalayas...!"

"Noo...Nooo! No Paarth, Krishna will never again meet me! I myself had indeed told Krishna..." as she was saying, Draupadi suddenly began wailing. Arjuna had never seen her crying so miserably ever before.

"What Paanchaali! What had you told Krishna?"

Apart from trying to bring back Draupadi out of her discomfiture, Arjuna started trying to find out something about what she had said....

"Krishna...Krishna..." drowned in tears, apart from these two words, Draupadi could not say anything. Taking refuge in these two words how many storms she had faced...but, today? "He who protected me every moment, I could not cherish even one moment out of that. Dananjay, I hope Krishna has not turned his face away, becoming sad because of that sin of mine!"

"Krishnaa...Krishnaa!" Arjuna became perplexed, as if some secret had been revealed...! "What...what...is this you are saying, Draupadi?"

Satyabhama too had become similarly miserable in the Royal mansion of Dwaraka, remembering something. Arjuna had witnessed her restlessness, her repentance.... Seeing Draupadi's discomfiture today, all that flashed back into his memory....

"Yes...yes...tell me, Arjuna, please tell me something.... Did Krishna forgive me during that moment when he had dropped his body? No...certainly not! And why should I deserve pardon at all? He must have never ever forgiven me. And where do I have the right to be pardoned?"

Not seeing any other way to pacify his wife, Arjuna gently placed his hand on his wife's forehead—It was as if wanting, to somehow compose her agony, and as if someone was wishing to give her support. Draupadi held that hand tightly—and, it became her support.

As soon as she became a little calm, she said—"The midnight of that eighteenth day.... Today even after thirty-six years, Arjuna, the great injustice that I had done toward Krishna on that very night, I am unable to forget it. It keeps piercing me. Arjuna, bail me out of this difficult pain; tell me just once.... Yes...just once let me ask Krishna for forgiveness, Arjuna.... Take me to Krishna, please take me. I fall at your feet, my Lord..." saying so she fell down at Arjuna's feet out of sheer fatigue.

Arjuna kept patting his wife's back.

The midnight of the eighteenth day manifested and stood in front of her—That moment of victory, of that great battle....

No sooner the memory of that midnight flashed, Arjuna began trembling.

□

10

It was the twilight of the eighteenth day's night of the great battle. One decision had been taken, many decisions were pending, many forces were active at various levels. The Pandavas had achieved the final victory. That thigh, which Duryodhan had half-opened that day, and called upon Draupadi to come and sit on it—breaking that thigh Vrikodar Bheem had completed the ongoing cycle of enmity, and put full-stop to it. The Dharma intent Pandavas had once again pushed back Dharma a little, with their greed for victory. By hitting his mace on Duryodhan's thigh Bheem had destroyed the dignity of Dharma, and, it appeared as if even Nature had turned her face and had refused to become a witness to this destruction....

Being touched by victory, the dharma flag of the Pandavas was shining even more brightly. The eighteen akshauhini army was lying shattered hither and thither. The entire Kurukshetra was lying thus spread out with dead bodies.... In that...let alone chariots—even men could not walk about easily.... Dead bodies, half conscious soldiers, moans of humans, scattered human limbs, broken chariots, broken bows...and arrows....

On one side if there was Kurukshetra, on another corner of Kurukshetra...in the camp of the Pandava army, Draupadi's five children and the brave brother Drishtadymna were in deep sleep. It was as if the fatigue of the eighteen nights, the afflictions, and everything else had intensified and fallen over their eyes. Since there was no more need now for the enthusiasm for victory, even the army was not alert as before.

Here Drishtadymna, along with his five nephews were lying in deep sleep and leaving them so—the sons of Pandu and Krishna had also left from there, ascertaining that there was no need for their presence any more in this camp.

Tomorrow, or early morning the next day, in the last quarter of night, the Pandavas were to return to this camp, and then the further planning for entry into Hastinapur was to take place. Their eyes were also drowned in the very same dreams.

The years of revenge thirst of Yaajnaseni Draupadi had also been quenched. That contentment was indescribable.... She too, swimming in that ocean of contentment, was lying in deep sleep in one of the camps, dreaming of a bright future.

The dead bodies of the eighteen Akshauhini army were lying in a heap. Wild birds were pecking at their scattered-cut-limbs. When they pecked at their eyes of the dead bodies, or, when they bit into the flesh near the heart, the blood which flowed from their beaks was black, and not red. Lumps of black blood clots could be seen clustered hither-thither at various spots.

Till yesterday those who were recognized by everyone...were lying today scattered like dead bodies of street urchins—there was no one to recognize them, except jackals and dogs, who were aware that a big eternal feast was going on to fill their bellies.

The moon had gone and hidden behind the dark clouds, as if having ascertained that he did not want to see this gruesome graveyard. This hiding of the moon, was as if children frightened by the awefulness of the scene, had gone and hidden themselves under their blankets...!

This great battle had completely steam rolled the earth. The dust raised by its fury had still not settled down.

Blending with the darkness, it was converting darkness into a deeper obscurity....

At such a juncture...two persons.... Wearing soot black attire, even in that cimmerian darkness, they were standing near the camp of Drishtadymna. Even this external darkness was appearing bright in front of that sin which was plotting in the minds of these two persons.

These were two Brahmins—Ashwatthama and Kripacharya.

Both, real maternal uncle and nephew.

Even in their own camp, the other real maternal uncle nephews were sleeping—victorious.... The defeated uncle nephew pair, had arrived, having plotted a conspiracy, in order to now convert their sleep into a sleepless mental form"—That fire of revenge...was desirous of turning everything into ashes....

"Uncle!" Ashwatthama whispered in Kripacharya's ears, "The Pandavas are in deep sleep...." Thinking the five sons of Draupadi to be the Pandavas, Ashwatthama was trembling with rage, and fire of revenge...!

"Son, this is the golden-opportunity to convert this sleep into their last-sleep...! We have given promise to Maharaj Duryodhan..." said Kripacharya.

"Yes, I remember, Uncle...!" said Ashwatthama in a subdued voice, tightening his grip on the sword in his right fist, and the mace in his left, "O You...the ones! who had destroyed the battlefield laws", by unlawfully striking at Duryodhan.... Get ready to taste the fruit of your Adharma.... Here I come...!"

At that time Kripacharya said,—"Who is the sixth person along with the Pandavas?"

"Possibly, it could be Krishna!" said Ashwatthama becoming excited.

"Krishnaaaa...?" said Kripa, as if a lightning flashed out of his eyes.

"Why? Are you afraid of Krishna, Uncle?" said Ashwatthama, who appeared just like Yamaraj.... The Rajasooya Yajna which took place in Indrapasth was dancing in front of his eyes.... It was in this Yajna, in the presence of all the kings rishis of Aaryavart, that Krishna had killed Shishupal with his Sudarshan-chakra—This scene was dancing even more vigorously today than before, even as it had many a time in the past.

And then...then that Sudarshan-chakra, coupled with that hospitality at Dwaraka.

Many things flashed in Ashwatthama's mind. That Sudarshan-chakra, on the strength of which Krishna had become the most-prominent person of Aaryavart, That chakra...can That chakra come into the hands of Ashwatthama's hands today? After committing Krishna to death along with the Pandavas...he...he...would become the Lord of That Sudarshan-chakra....

But...but...will he be able to take away the Sudarshan-chakra?—Ashwatthama's mind got a bit confused at the thought of this difficulty—For him, that Sudarshan-chakra was even more attractive than the kingdom of Hastinapur!

His teeth were grinding with rage.... Wrath, becoming his strength, was twitching today in his arms....

He reached the entrance door. In their anxiety free mental state after their victory, the sentries were in deep sleep. Something got entangled in Ashwatthama's feet, that even as he was moving forward, he stepped two steps back. A sort of terrible fire got ignited in his heart. Mustering all his demoniac strength, he leapt into the camp, and reached up to the sons of Draupadi—and...that's all...! after that...his mace started moving like lightning and began pounding.... He went on crushing everything that appeared in front of him. It was as if his animal hunger was not satiated even after swallowing everything. But, even as kept doing thus...he had not become devoid of discrimination.

Instantaneously, he realized his mistake. Those whom he was killing, were not the Pandavas…they were the sons of the Pandavas whose bodies he had converted into mere smeared human joint and that sixth body is that of the Pandava commander-in-chief Drishtadymna—

It did not take him long in realizing this truth….

"You! Preceptor killer!" Ashwatthama roared mentally, giving his last blow, and said, "O evil one! who had cut Acharyaji's head while in a contemplated state. This is the fruit of your lowly deed…."

Finished! Now no life was left remaining. Performing the demoniac dance over the blood splattering tender teen age bodies, he went on screaming mentally—"What if you are not the Pandavas? You are after all the sons of the Pandavas…. It was indeed Draupadi who had lit up this blazing inimical fire…and…and…into that very inimical fire…here…here…I pour in my offerings…."

He let out a wild laughter….

As it is the entire environment was covered with darkness…now it became disgust filled….

Something inauspicious occurred…a sound had risen… and…the sentries of the Pandava camp started running and screaming…. But…but…by that time…Kripacharya and Ashwatthama had already dissolved into the darkness, after fulfilling their vile deed….

When Draupadi got this gruesome news, flames burst forth from her each and every hair pore. She had lost her father Drupad on the fourteenth day of the great battle and now…even before she could take the first sip from their victory form golden cup, she got deprived of her commander-in-chief brother, and the future sovereign sons. That throne, to gain which there was so much longing...! even though it was obtained,…there was not even one son left to sit on it...!

The news spread like wildfire. When, along with Krishna, Maharaj Yudhishthir and other Pandavas arrived at the camp, there was a lull over shadowing the place. It was as if the cup of the victory-nectar had toppled over, even before coming into one's hands. With downcast faces, everyone was standing as if in a stupor. Ignited torches, quivering lights, dead bodies strewn over the ground… dust…blood…and this gloomy silence—! The entire scene was horrendous….

"Bheemsen..." cutting through the silence covered Kurukshetra, Draupadi's scream was piercing like an arrow. "You are the one who have always quenched my inimical fire. I have always been considering your strength as mine…O Bheemsen...! After sprinkling my hair with the hot blood from the hands of that evil devil who had dragged me by my hair and disrobed me, you only have tied up my dried-up hair after so many years…. Just a few hours back…."

"Paaanchaali...!" Yudhishthir tried to pacify Draupadi....

"And…and crushing that thigh which had insulted the honour of daughter of King Drupad and it is but just a few moments passed since you had shown your bravery by breaking the waist of that filthy minded one…."

"Krishnaaa...!"Krishna called out to Draupadi.

But where was Draupadi there to listen…? She was flowing away in some wind-storm, and was continuously blurting out—"You only had tackled the hateful behavior of Keechak in Viraat Nagar…"...her voice was trembling with emotion. Her long, soft, collyrium black hair, once again opened out and started dancing. Sparks of fire were showering from her eyes. Today, she was not ready to accept anyone else's existence—"And…and… Jayadrath...! seeing me standing as a lonely and helpless woman, had kidnapped me…at that time…at that time also. You only were there…who had rescued me...!" It was as if all the past incidents of life were pouring out one by one sequentially...!

Until now, within Bheemsen also, who had so far been standing like a statue, something stirred up and burst forth—

"Paanchaali...! I shall take revenge on these killers...! Within a very short time, the head of that son of Acharya shall be at your feet!"

Even as completed his words, Bheemsen had leapt up and proceeded to go outside.

And at that juncture, a voice stirred up....

"Maharaj Yudhishthir..." said Krishna, seeing the fury-filled face of Bheemsen, spitting forth blazing fire with hatred, "Stop Bheemsen this very moment...! Maharaj, to confront the war knowledgeful son of Acharya, we shall have to send Arjuna, and not Bheemsen...this work cannot be accomplished with impatience...."

Yudhishthir who had always respectfully followed Krishna's words, looked at Arjuna. Arjuna's eyes were rooted on Bheem, who was trembling with fury to finish-off Ashwatthama; hearing Krishna's words, he hands clenched around the bow-string of Gaandeev.

"Bheem...!" said Yudhishthir stopping Bheem, "Brother, what Krishna is saying is right...! Having broken all the rules of a battle, the son of Acharya has done such a heinous deed...! A man who has stooped to such lowliness...what more lowliness he will stoop to, who knows...? Hence, we have act with discrimination; Arjuna knows all the secrets of Ashwatthama's knowledge and skill...only he can give him a befitting reply, O Brother...!"

"Each and every moment is precious, Maharaj...!" Bheem started swirling his mace in the air, and its forceful pressure-sparks, began showering out it into the air. "Give me orders,... Until I do not place that evil souled one's head at Paanchaali's feet...!"

"Bheem...!" the solemn voice of Krishna resounded, "Do not forget that Ashwatthama's human-signs are already dead; that dead-souled Brahmin's head cannot change the results of the war, nor can he reverse this heinous deed...."

Krishna had hardly stopped his words, and Draupadi shrieked out like lightning—"Krishna...!...Krishna...!" Draupadi's piteous-tone was shivering, "The eighteen Akshauhini army lay cut and dead for achieving the goal; no sooner the goal was achieved you forgot Krishnaa...? You... you...forgot that brave commander-in-chief Drishtadymna, who had steered the Pandava army on to victory in this great battle! That brother Drishtadymna of mine, was killed brutally like an animal,...does not some thorn from that death prick you?"

"Paanchaali! Sister!" Krishna laid his loving hands on Draupadi's shoulder.

"Sister...?" Paanchali began trembling, "Yes, I was always thinking that if at all there is any sakhi dearest to Krishna, that is me only. But that was a delusion; today I have understood that between Subhadra and Draupadi, even in Krishna's eyes there is disparity, as much disparity as there indeed is between a right and a left!"

Everyone remained stupefied.

There was no noticeable reaction on Krishna's face.

The very same world-pervading compassion spread over his lips. His lips slightly twitched, slightly shrunk.

Maharaj Yudhishthir got up feeling uncomfortable.

Arjuna just stood staring blankly! "Draupadi, what is this?"

"What! What is this you are saying, Yaajnasenee!" stopping Draupadi's outburst, Yudhishthir expressed his discomfort.

"Let me say, Maharaj...!" All of a sudden, the Draupadi known to everyone, lost herself. By an extremely cruelest of strokes, she had become a son devoid mother...!

She had lost her balance of mind.

In front of her eyes, her five sons and brother were lying on the ground becoming dead bodies smeared with dust and blood.

"Why, Krishna?" there was a sort of contempt in her voice, "What you could have achieved in a moment,...why are you talking of evading it? Do you wish to give that killer Brahmin an opportunity to slip away into a more safe location? Perhaps...perhaps...there is a soft corner in you towards that son of Acharya...."

"Take control of yourself, what are you going on talking, Paanchaalee?" Yudhishthir shook up his wife.

"Yes, Maharaj, perhaps I just recovered my control...!" said Draupadi..."I am, unable to any more bear this dubious politics of Krishna, which I feel I am now visualizing. Perhaps, Krishna himself...incited this gruesome deed with some such intention that his real sister's son should get the rule over Hastinapur after the rule of the Pandavas...!" Draupadi could not continue further. Frenzy constrained her. Wailing loudly she fell on the ground.

All of sudden that camp of the Pandavas went lifeless—completely stunned! It was as if everyone had become deceased, although they were standing there surrounding the six dead bodies.... Just breathing was going on.... Piercing the darkness, they were a team of dead men, striving to find back their existence.

Yes, everyone indeed had eyes, which were rooted on Krishna.

There was that very same composure on Krishna's face—The same old! A sweet, tender smile which was playing over the lips, was hiding itself.... The quivering light of the torches were by now becoming steady—the shadows had shrunk,...had become small.

"Sister! Krishnaa!" the words fell out of Krishna's lips as if patting a child—"Look here, facing me" moving his hand forward Krishna gently caressed Draupadi's forehead. As if nothing had happened, he said something like this—"What you had desired…see...! that has occurred...!"

What was this being said by Krishna?

Everyone evaded their eyes, blinked their eyes…started looking hither-thither.

Bheem was standing as is where is condition.

There was no sign of Arjuna.

□

11

"Give up thinking about that fearsome hour, Krishnaa!" That scene of the past was becoming unbearable for Arjuna, "Perhaps elder Brother had spoken the truth only at that time...."

"What had he said, Paarth...!" looking towards Arjuna Draupadi asked him.

"Those who attained death in the great battle, they only indeed, are alive. Those who embraced victory, actually they have been subjugated."

Arjuna had been telling his wife not to remember the past, but he himself had never been able to come out of that memory.

"How one is getting elated at this victory when one is able to imagine that delusion today, then...."

"It is too late now, Dhananjay!" said Draupadi, "but even in this hour of great final journey, one desire does not leave me. On that dreadful night, whatever bitter words, unbecoming words I said, losing my balance, if only I could have prostrated at the feet of Krishna...." Draupadi could not continue further; her throat felt strangulated.

Krishna's feet appeared in front of Arjuna. Krishna's feet...! How can they be Krishna's feet? The feet of that body had...!

Once again a new repeat-scene surfaced up in front of Arjuna's eyes.... in the Prabhas-arena, at the confluence point of the rivers Hiran and Kapil, a lifeless body sleeping resting against the trunk of the Ashwatthama tree, and the feet of that body...struck by an arrow...! A life taking arrow....

"Become composed, Paanchaalee...!" striving to take control of himself—Arjuna said, "Here are the feet of Krishna, here itself...!—they are everywhere...! Try and contemplate on them, just once...! Spread out your hands, Krishna's feet will be within the reach of your hands…a live touch...!"

"Where are they? Where are Krishna's feet, O Arjuna" spreading out her hands in the air, she called out in a pleading tone. There was nothing anywhere...! She pulled back her hands and said, "No…Nooo…Arjuna.… Krishna will never again come near me. I had spurned him. Confronted by Ashwatthama's lowliness, I had become hysteric. But after all he was Ashwatthama,—the armyman of the enemy. Blinded by enmity and hatred, he had come that day, as if taking inspiration from a lowly bird like an owl. Perhaps his sinful-act may be forgiven; but…but, whatever I said—casting my allegation against the pure, stainless, compassion of Krishna—I had indeed become blind, Arjuna...! Why did you not stop me,…why...why... did you not stop me?"

"Unbecoming words and slander? The sting of unbecoming-words does not affect Krishna, Yaajnasenee...!" said Arjuna, "and that is why on that night, he told me to follow Ashwatthama, in place of Bheem. That night Ashwatthama was not a Brahmin—neither was he an army personnel—he was a lowly devil…Bheem would have definitely been killed at his hands. That weapon, which even the gods did not use in a battle, the use of which is prohibited by the scriptures—he used that Brahmaastra; and after that what happened, all that story is not hidden from you, O Paanchaali!"

"How can I forget that, Paarth...!" said Draupadi, Instead of the forehead of Ashwatthama, when you placed the gem in front of me, at that time it occurred to me—if necessary this gem may be returned to him, but—protect the one and only foundation of the Pandava-clan, in the form of

Uttara's embryo, somehow or other...! The embryo belonged to Subhadra's grandson—the blood of Krishna's real sister was in it...!; this matter had now become momentary; and yet…and yet,…despite all this…prostrating at Krishna's feet I could not say anything"….

"It is not that only spoken words reach up to Krishna, Draupadi. Krishna recognizes even the soundless word, and that is why he had fulfilled your desire, isn't it...? he saved us all from great sin of killing the son of Acharya, and that which you had mentally desired, he fulfilled even your that desire—he protected Utaara's embryo, and revived it...!" Arjuna suddenly recollected the past spontaneously.

Suddenly, a voice was heard.

"If throughout my life I have not committed any untrue action, then, O Almighty destiny! May the embryo in Uttara's womb come back to life."

Who had spoken?

How did Draupadi and Arjuna hear these words now here? How did these words echo from the walls on all sides?

"Did you hear something, O Beloved...!"

It was further heard….

"And if I have always adhered only to truth and dharma, then, O O Almighty destiny! May the embryo in Uttara's womb come back to life…."

Once again, a solemn, serious voice resounded in the atmosphere, and went on vibrating.

"Krishna, yes, O Gudakesh,…it is indeed Krishna's voice...!" Draupadi's discomfort increased, "On that fearsome night when the inhuman destruction created by Ashwatthama had begun seizing Uttaara's embryo also, it was indeed Krishna who had protected—these were the very words—did you hear, Arjuna?"

And again the voice was heard.

"And if I had never turned my back on a battle, if I had never ever done any violence, then, O Almighty destiny—may Uttara's embryo become alive...!"

These words were such, that they would arouse horipulations, make each and every hair stand on its end…! How could that voice be heard today? Each word twinkling like pearls, clear...!—same as they were heard on that night…. No...no…this just cannot be a delusion….

"Why don't you say something, Dhananjay?" Draupadi caught hold of Arjuna's shoulder and shaking it, said, "Are you hearing Krishna's words? It is his words that are being heard; and you say that Krishna is not amidst us now? You say that in the Prabhas-arena you had offered his dead body unto the five elements…isn't it…isn't it...Arjuna? That which I could not do on that horrendous night, that itself, let me do today at this hour of our final journey; let me place my head at those feet…." Draupadi's throat again became choked, tears started flowing like a stream, uninterrupted….

Arjuna had indeed emotions within him, but had no words. Something within was gurgling. He patted the face of his wife gently—his hands became wet. On the battlefield of Kurukshetra, that moment, when the Gaandeev had started slipping out of his hands...at that time also, his hands had become wet like this only. Out of that wetness, dilemma, despair had manifested; out of today's wetness, compassion, deep compassion is manifesting…. At the moment of that failure, Krishna had held his hands, today, in this wet moment of compassion, he felt absolutely alone...!

"Paarth...!" After a little while, Draupadi again said, "that gem which is embedded in Maharaj Yudhishthir's royal crown…" she couldn't continue further.

"What is there to be said about that gem today, Paanchaali?"

"I feel…I feel we may hand over the kingdom of Hastinapur to our son Parikshit but if that gem from the crown of Maharaj Yudhishthir can be returned to its owner…." The divine touch of compassion was spread over fully.

"O Draupadi! What you are saying?"

"It was indeed Krishna who had said, O Paarth,... 'A Brahmin, devoid of Braahminic principle...'—that indeed is the demoniac womb.... That son of Acharya's Braahminic principle, is now imprisoned in the royal crown...! This crown will pass on to the heads of the Royal lineage, and as long as it remains studded there, O Arjuna, till then no one can erase its history out of anyone's mind. And, and in this manner, until then violence, hatred and lowliness,—all these,—will be looming over the head of Hastinapur's royal-head, and will keep spreading all over the world...." ...it was as if Draupadi was fore-seeing the future; she was talking in a prophetic tone. That mental state which prevailed in her just a little while back was no more remaining.

"What are you trying to tell, Draupadi?" Arjuna fell into confusion, "There is no problem left now; we have to merely find a way to remove the obstructions."

"That is exactly what I am trying to bring up, O Lord...!" said Draupadi, "From forgiveness and compassion, the door to remove obstructions will open up...." She paused a bit, as if absorbing within herself, the limitless sky spreading outside, and then said again, "Who knows where the 'Braahminic principle devoid' Ashwatthama must be wandering about now.... There is an end to all this, Arjuna! The pain here, and the pain there can come to an end, Arjuna, if someone can return that gem back to him...."

"Paanchaalee...Paanchaalee...hope you are conscious of what you are saying?" Arjuna stood gaping at this unexpected form of his wife. Such a Draupadi was new even to him—it was as if he was seeing it for the first time.... She was standing completely far away from rage and revenge.... The one who was born out the flames of Yajna...from where did such coolness come within her? What has happened to Yaajnasenee—during the days of the forest life, during the incognito life in Viraat Nagar, in the royal assemblage of Hastinapur, during the times of sensitive incidents; so much so, till the morning of the nineteenth day of the war—

that woman who had always demonstrated collision, war and total destruction, that very woman? What was she saying now?

If at all...Maharaj Yudhishthir, and Krishna himself had made out some plan to prevent the total destruction, even then...that Draupadi...who had been making her own birth meaningful...who would have leapt up like a blazing flame...—this?...this...form of that Draupadi?

"Yes my Lord...! Perhaps it is only today that I have realized the Truth.... Whatever Maharaj Yudhishthir had said, its deeper meaning only now I am able to understand.... Proceeding forth on the great final journey, we shall all bid farewell to this five elemental world...but?...but... Ashwatthama? There is no such moment at all, in his fate, O Gudakesha...!

Arjuna once again slipped back into that hour of the past....

...it was indeed Krishna himself that had cursed the gem devoid Ashwatthama. He had said, "for your horrid evil deed, up to 3000 years...—you shall continue to remain alive in immeasurable wombs...without knowing the future...—experiencing the unbearable tortures of your own lowliness...!" How much anger? and how much deep reproach was present in Krishna's spontaneous words? How can they become an illusion now? Even if good deeds do come to an end, and may be forgotten also; but...but... this dreadful lowliest deed?—such a degenerated deed never gets dissolved. They remain alive for a long time, in order to caution the future generations about the ill effects of evil deeds—May be Krishna himself also, must have been thinking something of this sort only? Where can an evil deed performing person also get freed from this? He keeps burning incessantly in the fire created by his own deeds; indeed, a blazing fire.... This indeed is the result of an evil deed. Perhaps thinking of all this only, Krishna must have conferred the nemesis of immortality on Ashwatthama...!

"Among those who had it in their fortune to witness the era of the Mahabharat…we are final links of that chain. Now we shall all bid farewell. All these creatures, everything moving and unmoving, will be freed from its dreadful recollection; but only one soul will not be able to become free from the agony of this boiling pot…—only one shall remain, becoming Ashwatthama,…alone, tormented by this unbearable pain…." Draupadi was talking as if in soliloquy…"and that too, devoid of the gem, devoid of the Braahminic principle...! His unbearable pain will keep on increasing always—incessantly—each and every moment."

"Who has been liberated from the fruit of his deeds. Draupadi? Krishna himself, had indeed succumbed to the result of karma only; then how can Ashwatthama be liberated without experiencing the fruit of his karma?" Arjuna explained to her.

"For this immense and unending pain of Ashwatthama, for his this misfortune—yes I…specially I am to blame, Arjuna, I cannot ever forget this truth. Now when one has understood all one's faults and the time for erasing them has been presented…at that time…at that time…."

"What? at that time, Krishnaa...?"

"At that time, it comes to one's mind,…that, if by chance, may be not in this birth, in some future birth;…if by sheer coincidence, Krishna meets me and asks me—'O Krishnaa...! You have indeed attained freedom from the great agony of Mahabharata…but, the anathema which was born out of your enmity and vanity, and, has not yet dropped off from whose head…that Ashwatthama…even now is wandering about uninterruptedly. What did you do for him, for resolving his pain? This deed of yours…of wanting to keep the fire of your enmity and revenge, alive for generations to come…."

Draupadi lowered her eyes. "At that time...at that time…what reply will I give Krishna, O Paarth? If we can return the gem of Ashwatthama back to him, then, perhaps this self-inflicted pain…this sting of his own weakness… perhaps may reduce...!" It was as if the compassion of Krishna had come in contact with Draupadi's entire being….

"Calm down, Draupadi…" said Arjuna gently patting her back, "Not by the fear of Krishna, but, by the feeling of the contact of Krishna's compassion…may our lives transactions keep moving forward…only this will indeed be our supreme liberation…. We have attained this liberation even while in this embodiment…and with the support of this good fortune, may we accomplish our departure to the higher world, in the same way as here in this world...!"

"No, O Lord, Noo...! Let us pray that our higher world should not be similar to this world…. Krishna, the one and only Krishna, only he…other than him, may not any principle pertaining to this world, enter into our higher world…may all of us express only this desire. Take me towards some such destination, where all the memories of this world all the disappointments of this world drop off, O Arjuna...! The embodied Ashwtthama will keep continually wandering about in eternal epoch for that, what can I do? But, O Parantapa, take me to such a dham where we may not have to live amidst similar agony...! Now the restlessness is not to enter into bodily freedom but into some such arena of memory freedom...!" Draupadi went on talking under a fit of emotions.

What was this, which Draupadi was saying? These were the very same words, the same emotions, the same discomfort, the very same intensity...! How did Draupadi repeat the very same words today which Krishna had uttered? That spark which Krishna had ignited in the midst of the eighteen Akshauhini army, during the hour of commencement of the great destruction—about the attainment of a mental state…which, is still remaining in the form of a yearning...!—how did that very spark manifest out of the words of Yaajnasenee? It was indeed Krishna who had said…

न तद्भासयते सूर्यो, न शशाङ्को न पावकः ।
यद्गत्वा न निवर्तन्ते तद्धाम परमं मम ॥

Neither does the sun illumine there, nor the moon, nor the fire; having gone there they never return; that is My supreme abode.

"This is indeed that supreme abode, Yaajnasenee...! This is indeed that pre-eminent state..." Arjuna suddenly held the hand of Draupadi and started walking. He stepped forward along with Draupadi, to begin the great journey unto the arena, devoid of the sun of memories, devoid of the moon of affection, and the fire of desires....

□

12

Uddhav turned his gaze towards the sky. The smoke arising out of the Yajna kund of some nearby ashram, piercing through the thick collection of trees of the Naimishaaranya, was engulfing them.

Not even any one of the man-made pathways in this Naimishaaranya, was unknown to Uddhav. Perhaps in this close by ashram, the evening rituals of Sandhya, was going on. Uddhav took a deep breath. There was the sweet fragrance of ghee in the air. The mid-sky sun was perusing the earth in such a manner, as if some old man was observing his sinful son with anger.

The lonely Uddhav had been walking along since a long time. When, he had left, after meeting Arjuna on the banks of Bhaagerathi, he had changed the direction of his pilgrimage journey. That pending work for which Krishna had made him the instrument, that indeed…was propelling and steering him towards Gokul. He was going to deliver a message—the message of Krishna's body dissolving—And who was the one to whom it was to be delivered? Radha! Krishna himself had assigned this work to Uddhav—the message also and had considered him as the worthy one for that work also.

Time and again only one thought was arising in Uddhav's mind—When Krishna folded up the illusion of a body, even at that moment he remembered Radha...? Radha became Blessed! He shall now go and tell that blessed Radha, that Krishna is no more. How can it be said? What words shall be used? If the dialogue is ready in the mind, then only it can be said. And Radha! How will she listen? and how will she bear the dialogue?

From the day Krishna had left Gokul and come to Mathura, from that day Uddhav had been along with Krishna. Those days can never be forgotten…Akroor had come and told Nandji—"O Nand...! I have come to take Krishna Balaram to Mathura, for the Dhanush Yajna in the assembly of Kansa."

No sooner Akroor's memory rose in his mind, a bitter smile swept over Uddhav's lips. After the fall of the Vrishni clan, this senior personage of the Vrishni clan had accepted the serfdom of Kansa. All these incidents came up afresh in Uddhav's mind. A clan leader like Akroor had bowed down his head in front of the power and capability of Kansa—he had put a lock on his lips and later had also become a partner in Kansa's cunning moves. The secret that the wrestling match and Dhanush-Yajna was organized for killing Krishna, was not unknown to Akroor. Even then, that entire incident was very bitter. From the memory of that, bitterness started oozing in his mouth. Wishing to shake off that entire incident from his mind, he began looking here and there. He found his answer in a stream flowing nearby and got down into the stream. He had an afternoon bath. By the contact with the cool waters, those bitter memories got washed off a little.

After finishing his afternoon Sandhya-ritual when Uddhav opened his eyes, an emaciated, spiritless man was sitting on the banks in front of the stream, and slowly sprinkling water over his head. Uddhav's eyes steadied up. As if that steady gaze had touched him…that man lifted his face and looked towards Uddhav. Uddhav remained stunned. His eyes had worn out to such an extent, as if they were now two hollow-caves; and the face was so bloodless, that it appeared as if that of a ghost. He had worn the sacred thread over his bare body; even then marks of weapons and arrow-sheaths could be clearly seen on the body. Pressing his right hand on his forehead, he looked towards Uddhav. His lips began shivering, and body was trembling. And Uddhav.... His eyes remained as if being torn apart.

"Ashwatthama...!" said Uddhav, recognizing him, "This...this...state of yours?" The strong son of Acharya Drona, dearest friend of King Duryodhana, what is this that has happened? Only a mere skeleton cage of bones and flesh was remaining.... What a lofty personality was that of Ashwatthama and how drained out it had become and that is why it looked frightening!

"Uddhav..." his words also faltered, and Ashwatthama too staggered! And then as if breaking out his dilemma, he came back to his senses. Running, he went and prostrated at Uddhav's feet. He again stumbled. Uddhav lifted him up giving him support, and stood staring at his forehead for a long time. There was a deep scar.... In the abyss of that deep scar, there was foul smell emitting; it was still as if the wound was fresh in such a manner that blood and suppurate was flowing out of it.

Uddhav understood.

He had become devoid of his gem through Arjuna and through Krishna he had become an anathema and this Brahmin was reaping the fruit of his own devilish deed.

"Be blessed O son!" Uddhav put his right hand on the injured head of Ashwatthama.

Ashwatthama shut his eyes. This touch...of Uddhav's fingers, how much peace there was in those fingers, in that touch.... Ashwatthama tried for a long time to retain that peace, and then tears started streaming out of his closed eyes.

"Uddhav!" Ashwatthama's lips were quivering, "please let your hand remain for a little while, O Revered one! After how many years like after a succeeding era, I experienced this peace of an affectionate touch!"

Slowly, Uddhav moved his hand over Ashwatthama's filthy body. How many layers of sand and dust had accumulated over his body? Sliding from over his protruding jaw bones, tears started falling over his long flowing matted hair.

"Ashwatthama!" When he was a bit composed, Uddhav asked him, making him sit near, "After that dawn in Kurukshetra, today, after so many years your whereabouts is known, O Brother! Where were you?"

"Uddhav! Better to ask me where I am not there now." A slight smile spread over Ashwatthama's lips, but like a ghost! "That I should not fall under anyone's sight, I kept on running, wandering here and there O Respected sir! I had even forgotten to imagine, that I could ever meet such a human being! All of a sudden I got your sight, O Uddhav!"

Ashwatthama went on staring at Uddhav.

"Everything is influenced by karma, O son!" saying so, Uddhav let out a deep sigh.

"After whatever happened on that dawn in Kurukshetra, how much time has passed, Uddhav?" suddenly Ashwatthama himself now asked. A glimmer came about in his eyes.

"O Revered Sir, how many more years are remaining for the completion of the time span of 3000 years?"

Three thousand years? How many years are left for completion?

Compassion spread over Uddhav's face. Venue, time, coincidence—the limits of all these had gone beyond Ashwatthama—Perhaps after that horrible hour, it is for the first time he has met any known person, he was speaking to someone known. He had become one with eternal era.

"O son!" Uddhav said in a piteous tone, "There is hardly any difference between 3000 years and one moment, isn't it? Perhaps that moment also may not be very far off..." saying this, it came into Uddhav's mind...that he should ask Ashwatthama as to what all had happened to him in these 36 years? What all things had his painful feelings absorbed, and what all had it renounced?

"I have been wandering about since interminable eras. This is exactly what and how I am feeling, Uddhav! It is as if Time, like a serpent spreading its infinite hoods, is enveloping me.... Amidst the hissing of these thousands of hoods, an intense desire is left pending..."said Ashwatthama.

"Intense desire? Even now is some passion giving you pain? and...further...why are you further igniting the flame of this self-created pain?" said Uddhav exhibiting a little displeasure.

"O Uddhav! Till today whatever I did, and whatever desires arose in the mind, after knowing the futileness of all of them, now there is only one desire remaining..." said Ashwatthama, "Whatever I did on the midnight of the eighteenth day, that was so ignoble and vile, it was so despicable, that had not Krishna given me this opportunity, to keep on fanning this blazing fire of repentance, then,... I would not have got any place in all the three worlds....If at all I had been killed at the hands of Arjuna or Bheem, then my bodiless soul would not have got any place. And on account of the sins of the body, the soul would have had to suffer continually, limitless agony.... In order to uplift the innocent soul...Krishna gave punishment to the doer of the evil karma...this five elemental body only.... Actually I was not deserving this compassion also of Krishna, Uddhav...."

"Become calm, Brother...!" said Uddhav placing his hand on Ashwatthama's shoulder, "Let that past dissolve into oblivion. Just consider that it never happened."

"There is only one way. There is only one way to forget it, Uddhav!" said Ashwatthama, "If you agree to help me...."

"What is that, son?"

"O Revered Sir, should I tell? or not tell? I certainly have to tell, O Revered Sir, that please...I want to have Krishna's sight just once."

"Krishna's sight?" Uddhav became dazed—the colour of his face faded away. "What is this that Ashwathama is saying?"

"Yes, falling at Krishna's feet just once…I want to say, just once I want to reveal in front of him the sin lying deep in my heart's abyss, O Revered one…!"

Uddhav closed his eyes. What reply shall I give Ashwatthama? Krishna's sight? Now how will that fortune be available? Now only through the eyes of awareness he can be seen—He has gone beyond these skin eyes…—How can Ashwatthama understand this truth? And if at all he understands, how can he bear it?

"O son of Acharya!" said Uddhav cautiously, "That sin which is unceasingly pricking inside, that sin, loses its roots by dissolving in that very agony…. Don't keep brooding over that burden Ashwatthama!"

"Where shall I unburden it? I am getting suffocated, Revered Sir! I can get freedom from this, only when I admit another terrible deed of mine, in front of Krishna…."

Uddhav took a deep breath. "If this acceptance can be done in front of me, then, you shall be redeemed of that debt, son…." Uddhav was now unable to accept this pitiable state of Ashwatthama.

Ashwatthama went on staring for sometime. A dilemma…was getting stuck inside. He fixed his eyes on Uddhav, then his lips quivered, "Uddhav...! At one time I had conspired to kill Krishna...!"

"To kill Krishna?!"...Uddhav said with great ease, "That was a great battle, son…. In a war, for both sides to plan to kill each and every member of the enemy camp; there is no sin in that…."

"No…Noo…. This is not pertaining to war! Many years before the war—even while enjoying the hospitality of Krishna in Krishna's mansion in Dwaraka, I had thought of killing Krishna, Uddhav! In order to sever Krishna's head with his own Sudarshan Chakra, and, to become the one and only Vasudev of the entire Aaryavart; I had nurtured such a lowly and mean thought…."

As he kept saying, his eyes stood transfixed upon the blazing mid-noon sun….

All the opulence of Aaryavart, had that day, gathered in the Royal assemblage of Indraprasth. The invocatory prayers for Maharaj Yudhishthir's Rajasooya Yajna was going on. Bheeshma, Drona, Duryodhan, Karna, Kripacharya—all had arrived from Hastinapur. Here, great personages like Krishna, Drupad and Shishupal were also seated in their respective seats.

"Revered Grandfather...!" saluting the aged, knowledge-ripe Bheeshma, Maharaj Yudhishthir humbly asked, "The auspicious commencement of the Yajna is going on. Among all the eminent personages who are present here, whom shall I welcome first? Your instruction shall be my guide…."

Bheeshma cast his glance over the whole community present, and then smilingly said, "Son! In the entire Aaryavart, only Krishna is the foremost one, entitled to the first welcome ritual; is there any dispute in this matter? Performing the prime worship of Krishna, you act in accordance with Dharma, Son!"

The atmosphere echoed with the sound of instruments playing the welcome music.

Yudhishthir stood up. A votary holding the golden plate containing the welcome ingredients stepped forward.

"Stop, stop there…", standing up among the seated kings, Shishupal the king of Chedi, suddenly said in a grave tone. Everyones' eyes turned towards that sound.

"Declaring Krishna as the one entitled for the first welcome ritual in Aaryavart, Bheeshma has violated Dharma, and the propriety of justice..." said Shishupal in loud voice, "Krishna is not a king. He is after all a cowherd, a cowherd…. He who had spent his entire life grazing cows and calves, how can such an individual become the first entitled personage for the first welcome ritual? This is indeed injustice."

All eyes which were focused on Shishupal till now, turned towards Krishna. Krishna remained unmoved, and kept looking at Shishupal only; it was as if he was talking about someone else…such a detached look was seen on Krishna's face. He was sitting there, as if listening to some far-off sound.

"…in the presence of Krishna's father Vasudeva and Bheesma himself, how can the name of Krishna be uttered as entitled for the first-welcome ritual? And, Krishna has not even the slightest hesitation in accepting it also…. What lowliness...?" Shishupal was unstoppable today, and continued, "Maharaj Duryodhan and The Mighty armed Karna are present here itself. It is an insult to them also. Complete negligence of Guru Kripacharya and Acharya Drona…this is totally unjust…Bhagavan Vyasa himself has personally arrived here to accomplish the Yajna work. In his presence, this welcome being done by Yudhishthir is indeed mean...!"

The entire assembly remained stunned, as if they were mere puppets…. Only the voice of Shishupal was resounding over all the ten directions.

"…living in Gokul, he played the Raas leela with others' wives, the one who killed the capable King like Jarasandh through unjust means…." Shishupal's wrath kept on increasing. "Kidnapping other's wives, this Krishna who made them his own."

The smile glowing on Krishna's lips became more evident. Shishupal was hinting toward Rukimini…. Her brother had promised her hand to Shishupal, but Rukimini herself was not in favour of that alliance. Rukimini herself had sent message to Krishna, and prayed to him to save her from this alliance. Shishupal was not aware of this,… but where was there anything indeed, which Krishna was unaware of? Defeating Rukmini, Krishna had run away with Rukimini.... Shishupal was indeed hinting at that only….

"To entitle such a Krishna, to entitle a cowherd to become the first recipient of the first welcome ritual, is such a lowly act as getting a eunuch married to a heavenly Apsara…" roared Shishupal.

"Shisupaaal…" said Krishna getting up from his seat, and his grave tone resounded like some conch sound echoing from a mountain peak. "I do not wish that an exhibition of strength should become an incident on this auspicious occasion. In order to prove whether your vanity is justified or not, I am herewith offering you one more chance…. Preventing this Sudarshan Chakra's aim, you can as well attain the entitlement to that first welcome ritual...!"

Everyone was staring with wide open eyes. Perched on the right hand index finger of Krishna, the Sudarshan Chakra was looking radiant and intense like a sun. Within the wink of an eye, it sped in the direction of Shishupal. Shishupal also seeing this ferocious form of Krishna, was taken aback and dumbfounded. The Sudarshan Chakra, within half a moment returned to Krishna's index finger, after cutting off Shishupal's head.

The entire Royal assemblage which had become frightened and confused just a moment before, now resounded with victory calls of Krishna…. Ashwatthama was there visulalising this scene with wide open eyes. Krishna's Sudarshan Chakra and this frightened Royal assembly…. Something stirred swiftly within him, and retrograde vibrations started rising in his mind towards the Sudarshan Chakra.

□

13

The Rajasooya Yajna got completed unimpeded—The digression of killing certainly was an invective. All the invited kings-emperors, rishis and sages, beggars—guests—everyone returned to their respective locations. Everything returned to almost as it was earlier, as if a huge cyclone had come forward and receded but the storm which had arisen in Ashwatthama's bosom, had not arrived at any logical conclusion; his bosom which was surrounded by a mental dualness, was crossing beyond all confines.

There was no secret most weaponry knowledge left behind—the knowledge of which father Drona had not conferred upon his son Ashwatthama—the Vaayavyaastra, Aagneyaastra, Sarpaastra and finally the Brahmaastra. There was no Archer equal to Acharya Drona, disciple of Jaamadagneya Parusharam…in the entire Aaryavart. And that Acharya, had given his entire knowledge to his son Ashwatthama. Such knowledge which even Arjuna and Karna did not know, such Mantra-shaktis he had taught his son Ashwatthama, out of a surge of love for his son. But, that day, what Ashwatthama had seen in Yudhishthir's Royal-assemblage during the Rajasooya Yajna, which was filled with emperors and great brave heroes—that was superior to all knowledge. It was as if, within a moment, the blazing sun's spherical ring had descended from the sky, and, perching on his finger, had started rotating,—that countless rayed Sudarshan Chakra, had raked up a great commotion within his heart. He became very restless….

Grandsire Bheeshma must have announced Krishna as the personage entitled for the first welcome worship in the Rajasooya Yajna, based on some criterion. Is it because the secret of that announcement, is after all hidden in this Sudarshan Chakra? Within a fraction of a moment, it had severed the head of Shishupal…. And the entire assemblage of kings remained stunned, and looked like puppets. And in the very next moment, all the kings-emperors present in the assemblage, had raised proclamation of victory of Krishna. Surely, the power of this Aagneya Sudarshan Chakra must be dancing behind all these proclamations…. Ashwatthama's belief grew more firm. It was indeed this power of the Sudarshan Chakra only, that was making Krishna entitled for the "first welcome worship personage". It was only due to its power that Krishna was appearing so great! Whatever Ashwatthama possessed, who had that much? Who is equal to him today? But...but...this Sudarshan Chakra? This is what is making him inferior to Krishna!

"I have also got another Sudarshan Chakra, equal to Krishna's Sudarshan Chakra"; he had heard about King Paundrak of the Paundra region, throwing such a challenge...! This King Paundrak residing beyond Angadesh, in the neighbourhood of the Modagiri Mountain, used to say, that, he is Vasudeva...! "I have a Sudarshan Chakra with me also" was his challenge; but Krishna had shown the power of his Sudarshan Chakra, and established his Lordship, in the full assemblage having hundreds of people, and in front of everyone's eyes. Who had seen Paundrak's Sudarshan Chakra? But this could have been, merely his fanciful imagination….

There can be only one Vasudeva in Aaryavart...!

Today, such a Vaasudeva is only Krishna Himself...! 'Yes, he is'…but…but! Ashwatthama's yearning rose to a crescendo, crossing beyond the limits of the sky…it extended throughout the universe.

Once he becomes the owner master of the Sudarshan Chakra, and once he could get hold of the Sudarshan Chakra from Krishna…then…his dream of becoming Vasudeva, would not continue to remain an impossibility…. This is what goes on in creation…. One and only power…. Today Krishna is powerful and, that is why he is Vasudeva—If tomorrow Ashwatthama attains the same power, then, this very Yudhishthir will offer the first welcome worship to him, acknowledging him only, as Vasudeva—Grandsire Bheeshma will also praise him only….

But, to own the Sudarshan Chakra? It was indeed not easy to get it. That he could not become equal to Krishna,… who else than Ashwatthama knew this fact better? He had indeed seen that day with his own eyes…the thousands of radiant flames dancing on the finger of Krishna! And amidst those flames, how did Krishna appear? Totally immobile, compassionate, detached smile, that face of Krishna, he could not forget! He knew the truth also and also knew his own fanciful imagination…. This accelerated-yearning to become Aaryavart's 'One and only Vasudeva', was driving him higher....

There is only one conclusion, for the fulfillment of this yearning...—Krishna's exit from Aaryavart…. As long as Krishna is there, it was impossible for Ashwatthama's dream to fructify. There was no fear from Paundra's side, But…Krishna...? If his existence still remains…then… his dream of becoming the most eminent personage...and thus…becoming eligible for the first welcome worship personage…can never become successful….

Ashwatthama came to a firm decision. Mentally…he plotted-up his plan. Only by reaching up to Krishna, his plan could fructify. Enjoying the happiness of hospitality and fulfilling his planned task…with only these thoughts in his mind…he proceeded towards Dwaraka.

Seeing Acharya's son thus unexpectedly, in the form of his guest, Krishna accorded him the welcome due to his personage. Ashwatthama had already heard, that acknowledging the difficulty of surviving from the attack of Jarasandh and Kaalayavan…the Yadavas had fled from Mathura and had gone far away towards the west,…and had made as their habitation, the rich Kusha grass cultivated place on the sea-shore there. That the kusha grass cultivated place Kushasthali had become the beautiful Dwaraka, beautified with sacred prosperity and golden steeples…this was nowhere within the sphere of his imagination…. Seeing the glory, Ashwatthama remained dumb founded…. It was not as if he had not seen prosperity and plentiful; he also knew that all this opulence was of a fleeting nature…his eyes were rooted on the Sudarshan Chakra placed on a high pedestal in Krishna's mansion. That Sudarshan Chakra, indeed…was the focus of his yearning.

Once he could lay his hands on That Sudarshan Chakra…then this worldly journey of Krishna would come to an end and he will exit into the higher world. How simple was this task…. The farewell of Krishna from this world, and that too with these hands of mine...! After that, the Sudarshan Chakra will spin around the finger of this hand only. When the hundreds of eyes which had witnessed that Chakra in the Rajasooya Yajna with fear laden minds…see that very Chakra…spinning on the finger of this hand of mine…who then will hesitate to praise that sight!

"Madhusoodan!" said Ashwatthama. the guest, to host Krishna with great discretion…while the two of them were sitting in the mansion's hall and discussing leisurely..."Perhaps no one in the entire Aaryavart is aware of what knowledge of weapons, my father Acharya Drona has taught me…."

"Indeed your words are true, Ashwatthama…" Krishna said with great simplicity, "Acharya Drona is after all the disciple of Jaamadagneya Bhagavan Bhaargav himself…. Bhaargav has now withdrawn, hence, no one can imagine becoming equal to Acharya Drona."

"I wish to put this secret of weaponry in front of you, O Keshav!" Ashwatthama thus played one of his strategic moves, "Dwaraka is unconquerable, and you Yadunanadan, are its ruler", saying so Ashwatthama paused a bit. The sweet smile which was playing upon Krishna's lips was blooming still more.

"O Madhusoodan, if at all you could know the secret of the complete knowledge of these weapons, then even Indra himself, will never even raise his eyes to look at the Yadavas," Ashwatthama went on saying whatever he had in mind. At that juncture, Ashwatthama hardly had the vision to fathom the secret behind the smile playing on Krishna's lips....

"I am eager to offer this entire secret knowledge at your feet, O Krishna!" Ashwatthama had now started seeing the dream of his becoming Vaasudeva becoming successful and said, "in return you please accept my one prayer, O Madhusoodan!"

"O Ashwatthama!" said Krishna, placing his hand gently on Ashwatthama's shoulder, "Son, you are my guest! You are a Brahmin guest, and over and above, you are Acharya's son—who is venerable to me in all ways. Tell me, without hesitating, tell me. In return, without any kind of emotion, I promise to fulfill your wish...."

Ashawatthama started blossoming. He thought, that's it! now my dream is sure to fructify. There remains no obstacle.... Krishna had given him promise. Now within a moment or two, the Sudarshan Chakra glowing like a powerful Sun will come into his hand—and no sooner the Sudarshan Chakra comes into his hand, he will make Krishna himself its first victim....

Then, in the Aaryavart, Ashwatthama will be the one and only Vasudeva....

"So then, O Madhava!" said Ashwatthama become impatient, "In return for the secret of my entire weapons' knowledge, I ask for your Sudarshan Chakra...."

There was not even a flicker on Krishna's world alluring smile.... His voice was fully soft and unbaffled. Patting Ashwatthama's back, he said, "O Acharya's son! You want only the Sudarshan Chakra, isn't it? What is so big about it? In return for that there is no need for you to bargain with your valuable weapons' knowledge. As of now, I have no need for your knowledge when necessary, I shall make arrangements for it, O son! Go! from this very moment the Sudarshan Chakra is yours. You take it away from here, happily..." and then, pausing a little, Krishna added this much more, "If at all you can take it away...."

"The Sudarshan Chakra is yours from this moment...!" Hearing this much, there was nothing more left for Ashwatthama to hear. He felt as if drowned in an exhuberation. No other word of Krishna could reach his ears—i.e. what Krishna had said in the end...even if it may have fallen on Ashwatthama's ears, he had not heard it. He lunged forward. He stood up with the speed of lightning. Brushing away Krishna's extended hand, he moved forward towards the Sudarshan Chakra. With great uneasiness, he passed his hand over the beautiful Sudarshan Chakra. His each and every hair stood on ends—That's it...from now on I am its Master....

I, Ashwatthama, am the Lord of the Sudarshan Chakra. The eagerness with which he had pounced, that much wonder also proclaimed itself. He did indeed reach the Sudarshan Chakra, but no sooner he reached there, it was as if his entire strength had become exhausted.... The fingers which had moved over the Sudarshan Chakra was dangling as if lifeless.... A burning sensation was being felt on the skin. He indeed tried a lot, but the Sudarshan Chakra did not move even a wee bit.... Hope Krishna had not seen his childlike enthusiasm! A feeling of shame arose from within. Even without turning back, he tightened his fist over the middle portion of the Sudarshan Chakra a moment time. Forcibly, he tried to lift the Sudarshan Chakra. He got shattered.... Hope Krishna is not mocking at his failure? If at all Krishna comes to know his motive behind this, then...?

He once again tried to lift the Sudarshan Chakra with both his hands; it did not move even as much as the size of a tiny grain.... Ashwatthama was soaking with sweat.... That Sudarshan Chakra, which would perch on Krishna's one finger, with the ease of a flower...a great brave warrior like Ashwatthama, was unable to move that very same Sudarshan Chakra, even after applying his entire force with both his hands.... He made one more final attempt, but the result was the same.

Becoming crest fallen, he turned towards Krishna standing behind him. There was the same compassionate smile on Krishna's face and the same deep affection in his eyes. It was not possible to bear that face...those eyes... Ashwatthama lowered his neck.

"Son!" said Krishna coming near him, placed his hand on his forehead, "Sudarshan is Shakti, O Revered one! For attaining Shakti not Lordship...but surrender is required.... The day you come to understand this truth, even greater powers than Sudarshan will automatically come searching for you...."

Ashwatthama could not utter a word. In the presence of Krishna's towering personality, he started feeling his own individuality, dwarfish.

"Drop all shame, Acharya's son!" Krishna explained to him, "Any effort to attain Shakti, is not a matter to be scoffed at...but only the motive behind that effort, will decide its greateness or lowliness. Tell me Son...what was your motive behind wanting to attain a profound Shakti like the Sudarshan?"

Ashwatthama became restless. Should I tell him, that after attaining the Sudarshan...I wanted to kill you only?... If at all Krishna comes to know his mean motive of dreaming...of himself wanting to become Vasudeva...in place of Krishna?

In that case…leaving far aside the desire to attain the Sudarshan Chakra…his very survival would become difficult…. Without even turning to look at Krishna's face, Ashwatthama turned his back….

"Uddhav!" after opening an extremely burdensome chapter of the past in front of Uddhav, Ashwatthama's bodiless soul let out a scream, "In order to take the life of Krishna, I had meanly misused his own hospitality. Without understanding Krishna's large heartedness the mean attempt which I made to attain the Lordship of the Sudarshan Chakra...this matter…I can't forget this pain…. Take me just once to Krishna, I wish to give Krishna, the answer to that question of his, O Uddhav! Sitting at his feet, I want to accept my sin…."

Uddhav's eyes became moist.

"O Revered Ashwatthma!" Uddhav patted his forehead with great gentleness, "Get yourself detached from the dualities of sin merit, action inaction, Son! Ashwatthama is no more a body not any soul! From now on, let not any soul walk the path of mean lowly deed, may your life remain a symbol of this only…indeed…this was indeed, the deed expected by Krishna, O Brother! Keep fulfilling this expectation of Krishna."

"No, Uddhav no..." Ashwatthama said wailing, "Until I give the answer to that question, in front of Krishna, my pain will not get appeased."

"Now to see Krishna is possible only in the vastness of the universe, O Brother! Krishna has folded up his bodily actions…" said Uddhav gently.

"Meaning?" suddenly Ashwatthama became uncomfortable. "Uddhav! What is this you are saying? Tell me immediately, where is Krishna?"

"Krishna is near you only—He is here, he is there, he is everywhere—Krishna is now no more a body. He a supreme truth beyond the body! That is indeed what Krishna is now." Uddhav closed his eyes, "A great epoch has come to an end, O Revered one!"

"Bodily dharma.... Indeed to touch Krishna?" Ashwatthama stood up once and for all. "Without the drops of that affection touching Ashwatthama, the great epoch cannot come to an end.... The symbol of the failure of the great epoch will remain till this wound keeps flowing... until then, Krishna cannot depart..."Ashwatthama drew the attention of Uddhav towards his wound, "I will search out Krishna, Uddhav...! I shall keep on searching for Krishna...shall keep on searching.... May be even alone but I shall keep on searching and the day I meet Krishna, that day...." all of a sudden, Ashwatthama turning his back, ran towards the dense forest. The echo of his last words also, slowly became weak.

"The journey on the path of well being, is indeed alone. Uddhav! One may even get the instructions for merit, but, the Soul has to tread this path alone only. No one is responsible for anyone's happiness—no one is responsible for anyone's sorrow.... The lonely Soul and its deeds—only these two are there...they are interwined with each other...."

This cannot indeed be the cackling of the dry leaves under Ashwatthama's feet...!

Folding his hands Uddhav did bow to all ten directions. On the eve of the day taking the Yadavas to the Prabhas kshetra, Krishna had said these very words. That forgotten incident, how did one hear it again today?

Uddhav prayed for Ashwatthama once more.

The destination had come close. Mathura, which was situated on the banks of Yamuna, appeared...as if some beautiful and bright female cowheard had taken a child into her lap. No sooner his eyes fell upon Mathura, his steps slowed down. Even as he got into the blue cool Kalindi waters...he just remained standing in it. The sun was climbing down towards the west—as if it was trying to wash its setting-rays in the waters of Kalindi. The banks of Kalindi was without any people, and also silent. Apart from the medium sound of the waves of Kalindi and the chirping sound of the birds dipping their beaks into the Kalindi, there was total silence and peace all around.

Uddhav looked towards the direction of Mathura. Hooves of cows could be seen imprinted on the way—Here and there, the signs of the wheels of vehicles also were seen.

In order to refresh himself from the tiredness of the journey, Uddhav filled his hollowed palms with the water of Yamuna. Suddenly, his hands shivered, his palms opened out and the water slipping became one with the flow of Yamuna. What was in his palms a moment back…that,... now became dissolved in the limitless. Can anyone catch it a moment time? this flow of this water?

Uddhav once again bent down. Folded his palms and dipped it in the Kalindi—the palms became filled with water once again—one palm full of water….

Krishna must have bathed in these waters sometime—

Krishna must have performed sipping in the same water….

He had performed the Kaliyamardan getting into this very same waters—

This very waters, this very same flow.

The palm full of waters made Uddhav restless. His palms opened out again. The water again slipped out. It bacame one with the flow in such a way that it could not be separated again.

The cooing of a bird was heard.

Was it Krishna's flute sound? Where has that sound gone? Had the sound of Krishna's flute now settled in the throats of the birds? Otherwise, strangely, such sounds of the birds could never before be heard on the banks of Kalinidi...!

Why was the water of Kalindi slipping out of Uddhav's hands again and again? Hope Kalindi is not annoyed with

Uddhav? Uddhav stood with his hands folded in front of Kalindi, stood with head bent in salutation, and then...! out of the waters of Kalindi's flow, it seemed as if words were emanating—!

"O Uddhav! You had come here years back with Krishna, isn't it? Under the pretext of an invitation for a Yajna from Kansa. Akroor came here for the first time along with Krishna Balaram. At that time Uddhav! you were also with them, isn't it? Today how did you come along alone here? Where did Krishna Balaram stop over? To which direction did you send them, and came here alone, Uddhav? Tell, tell…O Brother, have you brought any message for me from Krishna?"

Uddhav trembled. Within a fraction of a moment, he withdrew has legs from the waters of Kalindi. What was this that the flow of Kalindi was asking him? Now it became difficult to look into the eyes of Kalindi. He closed his eyes. Few moments passed thus in total silence.

"O Mother Yamuna." Uddhav closed eyes opened, slightly. His lips quivered, "I am blameworthy, Mother! Leaving Krishna in some unkown direction, I have come alone to sip your water…. Mother, you will forgive this blame of mine, isn't it? But…but Mother, Krishna is uninterruptedly with you—Could you not hear the sound of Krishna's flute in the cooing of each and ever bird here? Could you not hear the footsteps of Krishna in the movement of the tortoises swimming here? When the cows shiver with the touch of your waters, at that time, don't you recollect the touch of Krishna? And…and…see Mother! These tear drops of mine…." Uddhav could not talk further. A pearl like tear drop slipped out of his eyes and dissolved into the flow of Yamuna.

Uddhav closed his eyes. After a little while, he said, "From now on, this lap of yours is the lap of Devaki, is Yashoda's lap. Mother Kalindi…now, this lap of yours, and…blended in the tear drop of Krishna's love, this peacock feather...—these two will now remain on this earth until the sun and moon are shining in the sky….

The water of Yamuna was flowing, as if it was washing Uddhav deeply….

When Uddhav had reached the fort gate of Mathura, it was evening…twilight time. From outside the town, the cows and cowherds were returning. That town which Uddhav was now seeing, that town was no more Kansa's; nor was it Father Ugrasen's. Ugrasen had left for Dwaraka along with Krishna itself. The Vrajbhoomi was always safe from the attacks of Jarasandh and Kaalayavan; that is why Krishna had abandoned Mathura, and majority of the Yadavas had gone along with Krishna to Dwaraka and settled down there. The remaining Yadav Vrishnis, and the new generation of Bhojaks had settled here; among that, majority had merely heard about Krishna and very few were left, who had seen Krishna and lived with him; actually they could be counted on one's fingers. After how many years, Uddhav had come to Mathura…that's it…. He would spend the night in Mathura; it was his plan to reach Gokul the next day. Meeting Radha in Gokul and after passing on Krishna's message, he would become freed from the bondage of karma…. Standing at the entrance gate of the fort, he cast his old eyes at the new township. Seeing an unknown traveller standing at the gate, two three youth came near him.

"Bow Respected Sir!" an elderly townsman greeted him, "You appear new in the township of Mathura…. Unless you definitely do not want to go somewhere else, please become my guest and, sanctify me."

"May well being prevail, son!" Uddhav said blessing him. From within, he felt a little uneasy. So even Uddhav had become newcomer today, in this township? How much had changed, in just a few years! Perhaps the same thing would have happened to Krishna himself and also, the townsmen may have asked him also a similar question….

Could happen, could definitely happen.... This sky, this land, this Kalindi—Even all these remaining the same... today, Uddhav was a stranger here. For the townsmen, he was a guest. Who has ever understood the movement of Mahaakaal?

"I desire to take shelter in some senior Yadava citizen's house, son...!" said Uddhav. A faint flame of hope was burning, that some elderly old man from Mathura may definitely recognize me.

"Elderly Yadava?" the questioner asked with wonder, "Among the Yadavas settled down here, the oldest is Akroor, O Revered Sir!"

"Akrooor!" Uddhav's hair stood erect. It was indeed Akroor who had brought him to this township for the first time. That Akroor is still there? Uddhav was wonderstruck as well as delighted. "Come, immediately take me to Akroor! After how many years I shall have sight of Akroor."

Uddhav stood up with emotion. During the period of stay in Dwaraka, and amidst all his wanderings,—he had become so much unattached with the past...it was no wonder that he should remain today, a mere unknown guest even for this township of Mathura.

"You...you? You know Akroorji?" that young man asked. There was both wonder and disbelief in his eyes.

"Son!" Uddhav said smiling a little, "Ugrasen, Vasudeva, Kansa and Krishna himself—along with all of them, this old man, had the good fortune to cohabit with Akroor also!

"Oh...! Is that so? You, you..." a group of townsmen gathered near Uddhav.

"My name is Uddhav, Son!" Uddhav placed his hand affectionately on his shoulder.

"Uddhavjee!" a simultaneous roar arose from the entire group. Uddhav's face was unknown to the new generation, but his name was not unknown.

Everyone moved over making place for the other, and one by one went and did bow to Uddhavji.

"Forgive me, O Respected Sir!" an extremely elderly man began the dialogue, "O Revered Sir, we did not recognize you! We made the mistake of thinking of you as an unknown guest in the trownship of Mathura. O Best among men, this entire township is your own house.... You have come from Krishna and Vasudeva, isn't it? We are eager to hear about Krishna's life incidents…."

"Yesss…yesss…" Many voices rose together, "We have heard about Krishna. You must have certainly heard Krishna's flute? Akroorji was once mentioning about that flute…."

"Please tell us something about Krishna's peacock feathers, O Respected Sir…."

"We have heard that Krishna had liberated the Vrajabhoomi from Kansa's atrocities—tell us the entire story of that liberation, Uddhavji! You must have seen all that with your own eyes…."

"Where is Krishna, O Revered Sir?" someone asked in an emotional tone, "We, from the new generation have been deprived of vision of Krishna with Peacock feather! When will this misfortune of ours come to an end?"

Uddhav's face withered due to weariness. Pain welled up in his eyes. Just a few moments back the peacock feather which had merged with the stream of tear drops, on the banks of Kalindi, had appeared as if swimming once again in the air….

"How come you did not see Krishna in this Vrajabhoomi, O Brother!" Uddhav asked composing himself, "Can you not hear the foot-steps of Krishna near the council chamber of Kansa? Does not the sweet tone of Krishna's cry behind the bars of the prison, reach your ears? And, even in the flow of this Yamuna, did you never have the glimpse of Krishna? And…and…. Seeee...! Seee there…look at the branches of that Tamaal tree and the Kadamb tree…."

All together, many pairs of eyes turned in the direction of that tree and remained steadfast…! they had been seeing these trees daily but…but…why is it appearing so new today? Never before was it seen like this…. As Uddhav was saying, how could peacock feathers been seen on the Taamal tree and Kadamb tree? All the leaves had all turned into peacock feathers…and…and…along with the rustling of the air, and from amidst these peacock feathers, the resounding of flute arose…. Were the peacock feathers and the flute, both here itself?! Yeess, they were here itself… these peacock feathers and this flute…indeed, Krishna is here itself...!

"Krishnaaa….Krishnaa…"

An echo emanated...!

From the courtyards and domes of Mathura, the echo of these two words kept echoing for a long time…!

"What is all this, Uddhavji? What…what is all this that we saw? And what did we hear?" great delight and wonder was spilling out from the voice of that elderly person.

"That's it! This indeed is Krishna now, O Son! The bone and skin Krishna similar to us, has now become pervasive in all these, Son! Krishna will never be seen in the bone skin form anymore. His mortal body has come to an end...!" Uddhav, ultimately spilled it out.

"What? the embodied Krishna is no more?" Everyone got a shock. As if a lightning has struck! The older men remained speechless! A few moments back, that Uddhav who had made them feel the presence of Krishna, that very same Uddhav, was now talking about the end of Krishna's mortal body. The townsmen became distressed. Once again their eyes turned towards the Tamaal tree and Kadamb tree—Krishna was here only…! just now. Uddhav himself had made them feel his presence. Now...now...those peacock feathers became invisible. Has everything gone and hidden behind these leaves?

"O Respected Sir!" one elderly townsman echoed the thoughts in everyone's mind present there, and said, "It was because of you only our eyes could feel contact with Krishna's peacock feathers. That the Vrajabhoomi Krishna did not deprive anyone, this also you only had told us…O Revered Sir! We were also being carried away by a delusion…you came and broke that delusion….

"We shall now be able to see Krishna in each and every atom dust of Vrajabhoomi, O Revered Sir! Come Sir…we shall take you to Akrrorji's residence…."

Surrounded by townsmen, Uddhav slowly arrived near the mansion of Akroor. The sun was scattering his final rays on the western horizon. The news of the arrival of Uddhav and the dissolution of Krishna's body, had spread all over the royal paths of Mathura as if being carried along by the flow of the wind. Leaving their respective work, the townsmen had gone towards Uddhav. No one was asking about Krishna. A deep pain was spread over everyone's faces, and their eyes were moist with the coolness of Uddhav's sight.

"Uddhav had arrived, and, Krishna had bid farewell"… Both news had already reached Akroor's mansion even before Uddhav's arrival. Akroor appeared extremely weak. It appeared as if the impression of all ten fingers from the slaps of Kaal, had left their mark on his face. He was sitting on a seat, right in front of the door of the main drawing room of the house. The hollow worn out eyes were bit restless—they were eagerly awaiting Uddhav….

Uddhav saw Akroor from far away, and with long-strides crossed over the garden and bent down at Akroor's feet. Only after reaching so close, was Akroor able to recognize him.

"My salutations, Revered Sir."

Akroor embraced him, "Son! the first time when I had brought Krishna to Mathura town, at that time you also were with him; today, Mathura is the same, is standing as it used to, and we two are also standing as we used to, but... but...Krishna is missing...Krishna is missing.... That hour when I had brought Krishna to Mathura..." he could not speak any more. Tears completed that work.

Uddhav's eyes also did cooperate with him.

□

14

From the fort of Mathura, when the sound of the gong struck, marking the beginning of the second quarter of the night, it sounded as if cycle of the time was calling out. The sound of the gong was echoing in the sky, similar to the waves of Yamuna. Akroor had become so run down, that the adult Uddhav, looked much young in his presence. Amidst this strange tremor, Uddhav and Akroor were sitting. Akroor was lying on the seat with the help of a pillow. The flags tied to the festoons were fluttering under the light of the torches, and casting their shadows, which were also shivering often. Even the town stood still, as if experiencing the peace and calm.... Somewhere the mooing of the cows and the rustling of the dry leaves of the trees could be heard piercing through the shivering winds. The flow of the Kalindi was hissing and moving forward, after lashing against the banks.

Just then a votary had placed two vessels full of milk on the teapoy and left, but none of the two had noticed it. Under the dim light of the lamp kept on the teapoy, the atmosphere appeared as if heavy and laden.

Uddhav told Akroor all the stories—about Krishna's dropping the body, the Yadava clan's renounciation of Dwaraka, the shameful defeat of Arjuna at the hands of the cowherd chieftain. Akroor in turn was absorbing each and every word in his bosom. Hearing about the last moments of Vasudeva and Devaki, his breath became as if standstill. And his eyes, even under the darkness, crossing over the long distance of Time, had reached Kansa's mansion and the domes of the prison standing under his shelter…and… steadied down upon them. The very same prison in which Vasudeva had spent the best years of his life—extremely torturous years…. Amidst the walls of this very prison, Krishna's birth had taken place…and…and…in the vicinity of Kansa's mansion, there, in that courtyard hall, the Dhanush Yajna had been planned and hosted.

"O Revered Akroor!" said Uddhav concluding his talk, "The path of destiny never stops! It keeps on increasing uninterruptedly. This moon, this sun, these stars and not only that, this Kalindi—all these are nothing in front of the cycle of destiny and not any better than these dry leaves. Just like the leaves of a worn Tamaal tree fall off and dancing in the wind fall to the ground, That's it…. All these are also like that only….

"Uddhav!" Akroor broke his long silence." See the colour of this Yamuna, Son! Its waters were never so blue ever before; even in the darkness of the night I had never seen her with such blueness…. Krishna himself was sky blue, Son! After Krishna's departure, it appears that his blueness has blended with Nature itself…see...Nature has become a little more bluish!"

"And that is why now Krishna had become pervasive in each and every atom of Nature, O Revered Sir!" The wise old man Uddhav thus consoled the very old Akroor.

"I am feeling envious of Vasudeva's fortune, Son!" Akroor kept talking within himself, forgetfully it was as if he were talking to the Yamuna river, "Going into Yoga contemplation, Vasudeva merged in the dissolution of the Yadava clan; even Yoga contemplation is not possible in my fate…."

"O Revered Sir! become calm."

"When I ponder with a peaceful mind, as to how I can get such fortune as Vasudeva's?" Akroor was becoming restless, "When it was the golden era of the Yadava clan, at that time, the time which I had spent with its two republic wings, and with the eminent Vasudeva and Ugrasena of the Vrishni clan.... Oh! What to talk of those days.... But whatever weaknesses or sins occurred from my hands knowingly or unknowingly...remembrance of those...."

"So what happened, O Revered Sir! weakness and sin are after all stuck with the human body's skin."

"No Uddhav...no! Vasudeva's existence was at first joined with the noble attitude of the Vrishni and Andhak clans, and then, that good fortune merged with Krishna, that is what I could not become...! and...and...that is why I am having to suffer this state of pain. I did not earn the competence for Yoga contemplation.... See Uddhav! Vasudeva gave birth to Krishna, and handing over that very Krishna to Kansa, I became a partner of the conspiracy of his death...when such things come back to memory, then even after many years that moment becomes unbearable..." Akroor's throat choked.

Uddhav did not say anything in front of his eyes also, Gokul was standing. That day, on which, when Akroor had come to Gokul, bringing the invitation to Krishna Balaram for Kansa's Yajna, Uddhav was also there only. Kansa's Dhanush Yajna was a mere pretence. The efforts of Kansa to kill Krishna Balaram, was not unknown, or hidden from anyone in the Vrajabhoomi. After disarming both the republics of Vrishni and Andhak...Kansa had established an unarmed rule over Vrajabhoomi—so much so, that he had thrown eminent personage like his father Ugrasen into prison. Everyone speechlessly remained looking...no one said or did anything.

And knowing all this also, it was Akroor only who had come with Kansa's invitation. After shutting up the voices of eminent personages like Ugrasen and Vasudeva, there was only one person left among their equals, Akroor...who was left free. Till today the Yadavas of the republic held him with great respect. Everyone was afraid of Kansa; respected Akroor...! The reason for this respect was not anything else—but the fidelity that Akroor had done to the republic along with Vasudeva and Ugrasen…all this was the result of that fidelity only….

Kansa was very shrewd.

He knew how to utilize men and Akroor also was not devoid of human weaknesses….

The quenchless longing for remaining recognized by the sovereign, had taken deep roots in him. He had tasted the power of authority. And, once that poison gets in, it keeps on increasing like the poison of a snake. There were only very few like Vasudeva and Ugrasen who had peeled him off like snake skin and thrown him; Akroor was not one among them.

All these were the wounds of the past; what gain was there in reviving them again? It would be good if Akroor did not recollect those matters.

"O Revered Akroor!" Uddhav said, "Those incidents in which we were the causes, surrendering them all at the feet of destiny in liberating oneself…lies wisdom…. Recollection is joyful, in the same way forgetfulness is not less joyful, O Revered Sir!"

"The arena of recollection and forgetfulness is out of bounds, Uddhav! Who knows from where a ghost would wake up and start calling? You will remain cheated—I am caught in its net, Uddhav! Acknowledging that ghost—I cannot survive until I submit them as my sacrificial offerings, Son...!" Laying stress on each and every word, Akroor said, that moment, when Kansa called me and told me, that moment…!" Akroor's voice got stuck up….

"What had he told you, Revered Sir?" Uddhav also sensed something new to come out.

Kansa had said…"Uddhav...!" Kansa had said… "Akroor closed his eyes."

The most unexpected thing had happened for the people of Mathura. The son of the ruler Ugrasen of the republic, had imprisoned his father, and had shown his thumb to the entire republic. The Vrajabhoomi was left staring at the incident, as if seeing a dream, and was left, as if cheated...!

Two eminent personages of the Vrishni-clan—Vasudeva and Akroor; the ruler of the republic of Andhak, Ugrasen! Combining with each other, these two republics, had transformed Mathura and the entire Vrajabhoomi into a veritable heaven.

But all of a sudden, something happened thus…that all this beauty was ruined; fear and imperialism spread all over the place. Yuvraj Kansa and his friends had usurped the power within the batting of an eyelid…Ugrasen was confined; later Vasudeva was also thrown into prison. Such an incident had never occurred in any of the republics of Aaryavart; such an incident had not occurred even in the Chedi, Magadh and Paundra regions. It was not within the scope of the Mathura residents to raise their voice against Kansa. Whoever dared to raise his head…his head was committed to dust. Again and again, one question raised its head in the minds of all the wise men—"what had transpired in the mind of the son of such a just and brave ruler of the republic like Ugrasen? Such a great insult of father? What could be the reason behind this?"

And then, some old man would say with a twinkle in the eyes, but in a subdued tone, "The ward of a mixed breed, from a woman who could not protect her chastity." That's all! then silence all over. Leaving the sentence half said, the old men would turn their faces. Everyone knew, that even the walls of Mathura had ears.

Only one was left…Akroor! he was free. Akroor was the only seed of hope in front of the helpless subjects. If at all anyone could do anything, it was only Akroor! If only he wakes up, and takes over the charge of leadership.... But this hope of the people of Vraj turned out to be vain. Within a few days after the imprisonment of Ugrasen, a scene, even more heart rending than the coup had to be seen by the townsmen—Akroor Maharaj, was seated on a high pedestal among the counsellors of Kansa.

Kansa was not only a leader in the army, he was also a shrewd politician. He knew the place Akroor occupied in the hearts of the people of Vraj.... He snatched the throne of father Ugrasen; he threw him into prison; but he had no hatred towards the Vrajabhoomi or the subjects of Vraja, behind these moves.... The goal of his attitude of enmity was indeed, his father...Ugrasen.

He wished to take revenge; revenge against his father... "His father had no justful right to rule", such a thought had taken roots in his mind, from the moment Narada had told him....

In the Royal mansion of Ugrasen and on the royal paths of Mathura, in the midst of the townsmen who had gathered for some festival, the manner in which Kansa had seen his own mother being dismissed...the better half of the Ruler of the republic Ugrasen—the crown prince Kansa's mother had become, for the gentle Aryas of Mathura...a rejected woman because...because....

No...noo...Kansa can never forget all that...!

That society, which could not honour Kansa's mother, that husband, who could not give societal honour to his lawfully wedded wife—"that husband, that society, that Ruler"—is in no way, worthy of honour, or worthy of protection...Kansa had resolved long time back—that I shall teach the Yadava clan such a lesson...that...that... these high nosed Aaryas...even the future generation of these Yadavas, will not be able to forget it....

And for this long drawn up plan, Kansa required Akroor; Akroor could become an extremely important pawn in his game of chess. Kansa resolved with certainty.

Even Akroor became wonder struck—so much honour? So much intimacy...!

He was given post in the ministers' group. What was all this happening? Where there was lurking fear, that after

Ugrasen and Vasudeva, his fate will also become the same... and...such welcome at the hands of Kansa.... Instead of fear and anxiety, he had started feeling a light heartedness, and also delight.... He is as useful now in the new rule as he had been for the old republic by the fructification of this truth, Akroor became more alert. If at all I can be useful to Kansa then, perhaps I could become the instrumental for steering this Vrajabhoomi once again towards the path of liberation....

And for this...it was essential that he should be trustworthy to Kansa; that he should be happy with Akroor's behavior and conduct then...and only then...perhaps the objective could be attained. To oppose Kansa was to invite imprisonment. The prosperity of Mathura, the dalliance of the Vrajabhoomi, this joy.—Neither was Akroor prepared to renounce all these, nor did he have this capability.

And that was the reason why.... the moment Kansa had called Akroor and told him—"Akroor! You should go to Gokul and bring both the sons of Nand...Krishna and Balaram here...under the pretext of a Dhanush Yanja." Akroor was left stupefied for a moment.... He immediately guessed Kansa's move. Inviting Krishna Balaram under the pretext of a yajna and then to get them killed at the hands of the strong wrestlers. This was the plan in Kansa's mind. Akroor knew that he was becoming the instrument for the probable unforgivable killing of Krishna, the son of Vasudeva; he began trembling even at the mere thought of this probability. Nothing could remain hidden, from the piercing eyes of Kansa. He immediately read through Akroor's dilemma, "Akroor, the residents of Gokul and especially the most prominent personage Nand...will not have trust on anyone except you. If at all the subjects of Gokul had accepted the Rule of Mathura, then behind that, the biggest reason is fear. Their mistrust for me is far from gone and over and above the havoc that Krishna has created there...keeping all that in view…it is crystal clear, that Nand will place his trust on you, and only on you!

"Maharaj!" said Akroor, as if his tongue had become paralysed. He had long lost the courage to oppose Kansa. And…and now? Krishna's killing? He had become shaken up, devoid of discrimation.

"Yes Akroor, this is my wish Akroor!" said Kansa in a commanding voice, "this is the command of the King of Mathura—Krishna will have to be brought here, no matter how...and this ever increasing fear will have to destroyed! Go…go…tomorrow morning itself!" That's it…the matter stood closed there. There was no courage left in Akroor to say anything further. All avenues had been closed.

A meteor had fallen on Akroor…and, cutting through the deep darkness, dissolved in the waters of Yamuna… as if in deep contemplation. Here that light heap got extinguished and there…from the fort, the advent of early morning, beginning of the fourth quarter of the night struck. Akroor was till now, amidst the pages of the past itself. After a short pause, he raised his eyes and looked at Uddhav. With his eyes glued on into the darkness, one wondered what Uddhav was looking at…. Everything was flashing past in front of him. In the dimly lighted royal paths…the washerman taking Kansa's clothes to the Royal mansion, the gardener taking sweet smelling flowers, the Kuvalayapeeth elephant and Kubja—going with the fragrant chandan ointment—everything was, as if it had happened yesterday.

"Uddhav!" Akroor called out. His voice was as if suddenly transformed. Even the silent-darkness stood as if it could not bear the burden of his call and hence, had become even deeper. "The very moment Kansa had included me in his ministers' group immediately I should have rejected it and then I should have commenced the struggle for establishing the republic. Instead of fighting open chestedly, I had deceived myself with the thought that "first of all let me become trustworthy to Kansa; then at an opportune moment in the future—I shall find some way or other. This conclusion was not noble—it was inspired by fear and selfish motive of one's own safety. In order to cover up this evil action...I began chanting Ganatantra with my mouth. Not by appeasing truth—but, by confronting it, and attacking it only—can one keep the torch of truth burning and alive? Though I knew this truth, even then, I could not pursue it accordingly...."

"Truthful conduct, is like walking on a sword's edge, O Revered Sir! We all know how difficult it is to observe this discipline of truth..." said Uddhav calmly.

"When Kansa commanded me to go to Gokul and bring Krishna alive, at that time itself I should have refused. As it is the stories about Krishna's exploits were reaching the royal assembly every day. In spite of that, Kansa, was after all Kansa, isn't it? He would have certainly killed Krishna if he had arrived in his royal assembly...there was not even an iota of doubt about this in my mind...." Akroor was squirming more and more under the burden of his sin, "And yet, I stifled the voice of my Soul.... Wherein conflict was unavoidable—there, I had accepted the path of conciliation. I consoled my mind saying that Krishna was after all a macrocosmic-personage. If I do not obey the command of Kansa, then whatever ill fate I would have to face that would certainly take place but Kansa would resort to some other ploy, and would certainly bring Krishna here. It was a matter of divine wish perhaps.... Krishna might himself kill Kansa.... In the event of Kansa getting killed at the hands of Krishna, then, the honour of having brought Krishna to Mathura may fall within my fortune.... When glory herself is standing ready to honour me then, where is the wisdom in turning my face away from it? If Krishna becomes victorious then...even on re-establishment of the republic, my place of honour would remain unchanged...O Uddhav." Akroor's voice became moist, "I...I...had become a full-fledged businessman, Uddhav! a full-fledged businessman…I extended my hand in the plot to kill Krishna; I had deceived the subjects of Vrajabhoomi, the innocent cowherds of Gokul and Nand himself; I had deceived everyone…I pierced a thorn in everyone's trust, and betrayed them."

"O Revered Sir!" Uddhav gently placed his hands at the feet of Akroor, "the trust which Krishna had placed upon you, that was indeed proved true in the end…was that a matter of less delight? Nand and the entire residents of Gokul had handed over Krishna in your hands—to you…Vasudeva's friend and the reverend father of the Anhdak clan."

"Stop, Son. Please do not say such words to me!" said Akroor in a heavy voice, "One had full faith on Krishna's capability and that he would kill Kansa and such auspicious feelings was also filled in my bosom but…but…history is not written with any emotions. It sees conduct isn't it, Uddhav? As it were, there was no such purity in my conduct."

Uddhav was becoming answerless. Almost at the fag end of a long term of life…the words falling out as Akroor's speech, filled with repentance and pain—were getting washed in water and was dousing everybody. A shower of eternal deep peace had spread between the two of them.

All of a sudden, Akroor got up and stood. His weak body staggered. Uddhav quickly supported him. Steadying himself for a moment under the support of Uddhav, Akroor stepped forward. At one end of the garden and turning his face towards the west, he buried the gaze of his worn out hollow eyes there, deep.

"Uddhav" he told Uddhav standing behind him like a shadow. "In one era, what was Kansa's royal assembly… there…there it is…are you not seeing it?" Akroor pointed with the index finger of his right hand. In the direction pointed out by that index finger amidst the numerous scenes, standing there even today, was Kansa's royal assembly... even after so many years…could be seen prominently.

Even in the cimmerian darkness of the night, the flag was fluttering on the steeple of this assembly; Uddhav could hear its fluttering...!

"Now the mere form of this assembly is to be seen, O Revered Sir!" said Uddhav, "but even after the passing away of a complete Epoch that unimaginable, hair raising and great incident to which I had become a witness... that fortunate moment...is still fresh in my memory. By the water which you have sprinkled over those memories which had withered away like heavenly flowers...they have again started blooming.... Its fragrance has started spreading once again in the air, O Revered Sir..." saying so, Uddhav became emotional.

Akroor was standing leaning on a bower in the garden and Uddhav, touching their green leaves with his hands was drawing the light from the darkness into his bosom.

The eight-faceted assembly had all of a sudden fallen silent. Packed to the brim with wrestlers, organizers and townsmen, the assembly had fallen silent. The blood stained bodies of Chaanoor and Mushtik was lying scattered in the middle of the assembly like broken down mountains. Maharaj Kansa's younger brother Sumaali also was lying torn apart by Balaram's plough, in an almost dead state. Witnessing this frightsome scene, sitting in the half-crescent shaped stadium seats, the Yadava women were shrieking. That the end of these two cowherd boys' is near at hand, no one had any doubt at all about this...! The golden jar filled with costly wine, pillars—shining like a mountain peak and flower petal sprinkled seats—everything had fallen silent.... Reaching the midnoon overhead the sun also remained steady as if staring at the Mathura township.

Hundreds of people saw Kansa trembling with enmity and rage. The awesome roar that emanated from his throat was also heard by everyone and shivering with fright all eyes turned towards Krishna. The expression of emotion which could be seen on Krishna's face, such an expression!

the residents of Mathura had never seen before! No enmity, nor excitement, neither any bewilderment.... Neither any sign of anxiety; such an alluring smile, filled with love and compassion—no one had ever seen such a smile ever before. Such a sweet smile and that too at this fearsome hour? how was this possible? Alas! this smile is after all only for a fraction of a moment!—understand that its end had neared now.... Indeed...how can this tender peacock feather, stand in front of the brute animal strength of Kansa?

All of a sudden a lightning struck. Such a powerful light spread, that eyes became blinded. People forcibly squeezed their eyes in an effort to see, and their eyes became as if torn apart. A tremendous sound emanated. From some corner of the assembly great scream was heard. Some saw, some did not see and what was being considered impossible that had occurred—Kansa's hair was in Krishna's hands and he was vomiting blood right in the middle of the assembly. Kansa was rolling in the dust under the throne. His golden crown was lying in the blood and holding his long silky hair in his fist, Krishna was dragging his body.

What an unimaginable scene it was?

Kansa's mouth was full of froth. His body started stretching. His studded ornaments scattered all over. Like the stormy waves of an ocean, there was mayhem in the assembly. Just a few hours back those who had seen Krishna tearing apart the huge elephant Kuvalayapeed with his own tusk, now. Their hair got goose-bumps, as they stood staring at this fearsome scene.... Just like a small holy basil plant growing beside a huge fig tree, Krishna was standing near Kansa who was squirming on the ground. From deep within the harem beyond the stadium, the piteous wailing of women could be heard.

"Uncle!" bending a little, and taking his mouth near Kansa's ear, Krishna shouted. Krishna's peacock feather was touching Kansa's cheek. The feel of this peacock feather, revealed itself in Kansa's eyes, "In the Law of destiny, I have merely become an instrument Uncle! Leaving behind enmity and hatred here itself, may you begin your journey for the attainment of the Supreme!"

"Krishna..." said Kansa in a weak voice. There was the echo of death coming out of his voice. The moment this voice arose, the crowd which was making victory sounds, suddenly fell silent. Kansa was still alive!

"Both the sides…mother's as well as father-in-law's sides are equally authorised to perform the last rites like that of the father's side itself, O Uncle!" said Krishna. "Knowing this also I have had to become the instrument on account of an inevitable fate!"

"The law of creation ended here, O Krishna!" said Kansa gasping for breath, "in such a creation, both victory and defeat are inevitable. I am not so ignorant that I cannot understand this truth—but…."

"Say it unhesitatingly, O Uncle!" said Krishna affectionately.

"Narada had told me" said Kansa, and stopped a little.

"What had Narada told, Uncle?"asked Krishna.

Such a quietness had spread all over the assembly, that even the hissing of the wind could be heard.

"Narada had told me, that your death is certain to take place at the hands of Devaki's eighth son!" Opening up a page from the past, Kansa·was gazing at the sky, "In order to save myself from that probable destruction, I tried my best to kill the foetus in Devaki's womb itself, Krishna! My enmity towards you was enmity, if one considers it to be so, or else it was the result of a natural reaction of human beings. I had made many efforts to destroy you, to kill you; because…I myself wanted to live! There was this natural human reaction behind my efforts to kill you. I was inspired by Davarshi Narada's prophetic words…." Kansa again got choked. Blood was continually flowing out of his wounds. Taking respite for a while, he again said forcefully, "But, O Krishna! but…what mission are you talking of, in this effort of yours to bring about my death; I am unable to understand this mission of yours for the sake of my destruction? Your hatred towards me."

"Don't call it hatred, Uncle!" said Krishna interrupting him in the middle, "You had bound yourself to trespass over the prophetic words of Devarshi Narada…and I…I… wished to become an instrument for the re-establishment of republics."

"You mean?"

"This is what you did to the noble traditional heredity of the Aaryas—You destroyed the traditional republic of Vrajabhoomi. For the welfare of the majority, for the happiness of the majority; you steam rolled, this pledge of a Republican council. You could not contain your lust for governance."

"Krishna!" an understandable smile came over Kansa's face, "Imperialism is not any new tradition. Even the Aarya clan is not unfamiliar with it. 'That republic… that republic.'?" Kansa's lips became twisted, his eyes were showering burning cinders. His eyebrows tensed up, "That republic has rotted, that republic…in which innocent, sinless women are not honoured that republic…the eminent personages of that republic, who revelling in the glory of their own fame.—outcasts even one's own wife."

"What are you talking, Uncle?" said Krishna placed his hand on Kansa's blood stained forehead and cast his gaze on the society standing silently nearby—the heads of the elderly members of the council bent down.

"Krishna!" said Kansa in a somewhat raised voice. He vomited blood from his mouth, as if he was spitting on the faces of the elderly men, "Ask these protectors of the republic just once, whether these people acknowledged my mother as scorn worthy? Why was she rejected in such a manner? That woman who was completely sinless, she was a chaste woman…slandering the holy demeanor of that woman, why did her husband reject her? That husband, who cannot protect the honour of his own wife, does he have the right to rule over a republic?"

Krishna's eyes roved all around over the entire society men—no one raised his head and looked up. Krishna's eyes returned answerless...!

"None among these will talk, Krishna...!" said Kansa, "All these people are spineless.... When the republic came to an end, these people shouted my triumph. Now all these people will shout your triumph. That day when the ruler of the republic Ugrasen, outcast his dharmapatni—and pronouncing slander on the character of my mother, devalued my birth...in that hour, there were locks on the mouths of all these people.... These cowards, who had never accepted me in the form of a Yadava, these cowards are afraid of me even now...."

"Uncle...uncle! The one who says you are not a Yadava, is a sinner...."

"Krishnaa...!" suddenly Akroor's voice could be heard in the middle. Krishna's sentence remained unfinished. "There is partial truth in Kansa's words, O Keshav! Kansa's mother...."Akroor turned and looked towards Kansa. The shadow of death could be seen clearly on Kansa's face.

"Don't afraid, Akroor!" said Kansa, "If anyone had mustered up courage to speak out thus even an hour back, then his head would have fallen on earth severed from his trunk. But...but...now...now...tell Krishna! O Revered Sir! how Kansa's sinless mother was declared a sinner by this republic of yours.... Also tell how Kansa...made this woman, who was established as a sinner...to be acclaimed honourable by the state, to be acceptable by people—Tell... tell all this, O Revered Sir!" As he was saying this, Kansa closed his lips tightly....

□

15

The entire assembly hall filled with people was still, like some cursed stone statue. Hiccups, subdued sighs, were some sounds that could be heard. The great-powerful Kansa was still alive. The cowherd boy Krishna of Gokul was also in front of him, and all the elderly citizens were looking at both of them. Indeterminate, confusion prevailed—Far away from death, the defeat of Kansa is also impossible; till today such had been the conclusion. The ability to defeat Kansa was in only in the hands of Akroor and that Akroor was Kansa's most politically acknowledged minister—and once again the rebirth of a republic? That thought was not there even in anybody's dream…and here…an unknown cowherd boy's hand knocking at the door of a Republic.... Everyone had even forgotten to wink their eyes.

"Maharaj Kansa!" Akroor addressed Kansa so that everyone could hear him, "Leaving behind the memories of this world one has to proceed on the journey to the higher world. Whatever father Ugrasen had done during that moment, after all that was also only to protect the honour and dignity of the Yadava clan."

"During these last moments, please do not make me listen to such babbling" said Kansa in a loud voice, mustering all his strength "That fatherhood, which Ugrasen himself also did not acknowledge, you are connecting honour and dignity against the name of that fatherhood? In the name of Republic, this is nothing but the vanity doctrine of a handful of people like you…." Kansa could not speak further. After all, how much more force was left in his breath? After halting a while, he looked towards Krishna and then spoke slowly, "Krishna! Perhaps you are thinking that this excitation of mine has arisen from my faint heartedness of an impending defeat! But it is no so Krishna! Kansa can digest defeat also in the same manner in which he can embrace victory!" And suddenly facing Akroor, he roared in the voice of a power holding ruler, "Akroor! Maharaj is still alive…and this Maharaja of Mathura commands you…to tell Krishna…that the Republic about which he has been raving that republic, the ruler of that republic…had told that the chastity and womanhood of even an innocent and sinless woman should be established. Tell him Akroor…tell him…before my breath stops, let me recollect that hour once again."

Magadh, Chedi and Paundra—like Imperialistic empires towards the east and a strong kingdom like Hastinapur towards the North west. Thus in the Vrajabhoomi surrounded on three sides in this manner, the Yadava Republic shone like a small bright flame, replacing a One man rule…for the benefit of the majority and for the happiness of the majority. Even though surrounded by the strong empires…the eminent personages of Andhak and Vrishni—were protecting the bright republic of this piece of land and protecting its tradition. The tradition of Republics in other regions had more or less become unsuccessful and all clans had more or less accepted their respective emperors.... Only the Vrajabhoomi and the Yadava families had preserved the values of their ancestral tradition and no sounds of individual victory would be raised. There was reverence for the Rule…not fear….

To the south of Mathura, the mountain Suyaamun, and its nearby beautiful green shrubbery, was the extremely favourite recreation spot of Ugrasen and his wife Pavanrekha. As soon as he got some spare time from governance, Ugrasen along with Pavanrekha would reach out into the dense forests of Suyaamun, and would seek peace amidst the creepers and bowers there.

That day also, husband wife was thinking of going to nature's abode of Suyaamun, when suddenly due to some urgent work, Ugrasen had to stay back. Pavanrekha became a little disappointed.

"No dear, why do you become sad?" said Ugrasen guessing her sadness, "You go ahead with few votaries to that spot, our favourite place. Settling this important work, rest assured that I shall come just behind you."

Pavanrekha blossomed with joy. What is more joyful than waiting for her husband amidst the gardens! With a few friends of hers, she reached the Suyaamun mountain valley. Just adjacent to her most favourite spot there was a clear water stream flowing. Pavanrekha and her friends entered this nature's abode, and were free from any restrictions. Before Aarya Ugrasen could arrive, everyone entered into the stream with the intention of bathing and playing water sports. Both body and mind were free from all coverings.... Water sports, delightful screaming, splashing water on each other...thus unrestricted and completely engrossed in these sports, these women did not even have any clue that the king of Saubh, Durmil, was observing their beauty hiding behind the bushes.

Durmil was not an emperor. He was known merely as a name sake in the Aaryavart; he neither possessed such wealth power, or fame. He was governing happily within the limited land of Saubh. Amidst the victory cries of the empires, possibly no one's attention was drawn towards Durmil and his Saubh township and Durmil also was least interested in expanding the limits of his rule. By diligently observing his peaceful daily routine, he was able to attain a wondrous knowledge.... With that knowledge, he would be able to assume a illusory form. Whenever required he would be able to assume any desired form. An ordinary human being gets oppressed by great desires after attaining such capability; however fortunately Durmil was free from them.

Today he also, wandering about for pleasure reached this spot. His eyes were absorbed in drinking the pure beauty of Nature, when suddenly the body of a bathing beauty distracted his attention; something sprouted within him, seeing such beauty. Such attraction. Whatever Durmil had never ever seen before…that…appeared before his eyes...such restlessness as he had never experienced ever before that started making him lose his self control. It was as if a dark line had got imprinted on the sinless pure face of Nature. Durmil allowed himself to be sucked in by its flow….

"Maharaj!" he was startled by the sound of one of his attendants. "The head of the Mathura republic, Aarya Ugrasen is on his way and will reach here in a short while; such a message has been brought by our messenger."

"Ugrasen? Here? and now?" Durmil was talking, but his eyes were still absorbed by that very beautiful body silhouette; otherwise what interest did he have in the news of Ugrasen's arrival?

The attendant passed on the next part of the message—"It is heard that on that side near some stream, his wife Pavanrekha is waiting for her husband in the creeper bower.

Got it…Durmil got the introduction; so that was the name of that unrestricted disrobed beautiful damsel… Pavanrekha "Oh! so this is Arya Ugrasen's extremely beautiful wife Pavanrekha?" A moment back the message brought by the messenger which had been tasteless, that very same message now gave Durmil peace.

"You all go and make preparations for the journey. "Durmil ordered the attendant, "I shall follow…just in a short while…."

The moment the attendants were out of sight there... here…Durmil made up his mind. He closed his eyes. There was a moment's total silence...and when he opened his eyes, there was no Durmil—Ugrasen was there! And there was a cunning smile on his face…would Pavanrekha accept him now? Indeed...no one will be able to recognize his Durmil form.

He quickly got down and walked straight towards the stream. He was able to see the nude bathing Pavanrekha, whom he now wanted to see closely.

No sooner the free bathing Pavanrekha and her friends saw Ugrasen coming down the Mathura path alone with quick steps, everyone felt ashamed that Ugrasen would reach so soon and that too alone? No one had indeed even imagined this! Durmil was clever. He had taken the form of Ugrasen and not only that he also copied Ugraen's behavior. As if he had suddenly come across this bathing scene, he stopped and turned his face and stood.

The shameful friends of Pavanrekha took advantage of this opportunity! Picking up their clothes, they ran far away under cover of the creeper bower. Pavanrekha too was certainly taken a back; somehow or the other draping clothes around her body, shaking her hair off from the water, she reached near her husband.

"You came very soon, Lord?" she asked lovingly.

Durmil remained quiet. He can certainly deceive by his face, but not by his voice; there was wisdom in keeping silent! He pulled Pavanrekha towards him with a jerk…the Pavanrekha who was standing bashfully in sparse clothes and with a hesitating look….

Pavanrekha raised her eyes towards him—she saw a mad agitated face before her. That lustful eager look on her husband's face, excited her also for a split moment. She embraced a devilish barber Durmil.

"Oh Lord! What a sweet…joyful moment this is!" Pavanrekha's breathing was becoming sporadic; with half open eyes, she could hardly see Ugrasen. Durmil completely enveloped her body by his own. Time remained stupefied.

One moment, two, three, four moments…suddenly Pavanrekha woke up with a start like a lightning she got up with a jerk and stood up. Ugrasen...? Her husband Ugrasen?

Today…today…what has happened to him? Like this…like this...? He had never ever crushed the tender body of his wife, so harshly!

She was startled! Ugrasen...? What has happened today to Aarya Ugrasen? All of a sudden she started sensing him to be a stranger.... But...but...by that time…it was too late!

"You…you? what…what…what is this you are doing? What has happened to you?" said a panting Pavanrekha in a broken up voice, full of fear. Her eyes were getting dimmed with agitation.

"I am indeed blessed today, O Sundari." Durmil spoke up for the first time and…it was if the sky had exploded!

Pavanrekha let out a shriek, "You?…you…who are you? She tried to cover herself with a few clothes but...her trembling did not stop.

"Those moments which we had together, those moments will always be with me." Durmil said laughing, "That is my introduction, that is my name! The joy which you have given me."

"You sinner!" Pavanrekha fell down becoming weak, "You bad charactered man! You…you…you have polluted my chastity…" and her voice was drowned in her weeping.

"Polluted?" Durmil guffawed loudly, "You are very innocent, Sundari! You indeed did think of me as your husband Ugrasen and that is why you surrendered your body; then how can you be said to be polluted? And this union, is nothing but a mere natural incident, isn't it?"

Darkness spread around Pavanrekha's eyes. She stumbled and fell. When she got back her consciousness, Aarya Ugrasen and the friends who had accompanied her to the forest sport came along with him and were standing there; the half clothes on her body and her crumpled up clothes and also her mannerism spoke volumes for what had happened; they understood everything.

Coming out from the water when Pavanrekha had gone towards Durmil, thinking him to be Ugrasen…the friends accompanying her had gone away under the cover of the creeper bowers. As they were wearing their clothes properly there…and just after a little while…her friends saw Ugrasen with his attendants coming from the direction of Mathura... but…this time…leaving the main path they had seen him coming crossing over the ups and downs of the path. They fell into a dilemma. Just a few moments back, they had seen Ugrasen coming via the main path, all alone...Pavanrekha also, went near her husband...and now...from this different direction? Aarya Ugrasen coming from a different direction with his attendants? What a strange spectacle? Ugrasen also saw this group of friends of Pavanrekha and seeing Pavanrekha not there with them, was astonished and also got worried. Going near them, he asked regarding this.

"Forgive us Aarya." One elderly woman said, "It was just now that you had come via the main path towards the stream; we all came here under cover of the creeper bowers and Pavanrekha Devi came near you…have you forgotten?"

Ugrasen remained stunned. Now it seemed…as if these women also had started recollecting something. That Ugrasen, near whom they had left Pavanrekha and come here…his attire was not like this Ugrasen.... What had happened? What is all this?

Ugrasen walked swiftly towards that stream.

On the banks of the stream under the cover of a creeper Pavanrekha was lying half conscious, in a half nude state!

She opened her eyes. No sooner her eyes fell on the people who stood surrounding her, suddenly she got up and stood, with a jerk. Draping her clothes somehow or other, she covered her shame, and quickly went under the cover of the trunk of a tree. Everyone looked at Ugrasen…. They were as if dazed! could not understand anything, nor could say anything…they were as if inert! The crowd dispersed and both were left alone now. After remaining in a state of confusion for a while, Ugrasen now moved from his place, and reached near the shriveling

Pavanrekha, who was standing under the cover of the tree. She was unable to lift her eyes; she was neither able to say anything.

Indeed and after all this occasion had to be put an end to. "Pavanrekha, the present generation of the republic may perhaps ignore this matter, but how will the future generation react to this 'chastity depraving' incident of the wife of the Ruler of their Republic, Ugrasen? This decline in the chastity of a woman…this chastity, which has been our traditional and cultural heredity…will turn out to be, the first rung in the ladder of downfall of both the Vrajabhoomi and the republican state!"

"I am innocent Master, I am sinless...!" saying so Pavanrekha fell at the feet of her husband. Apart from the sound of wailing and crying, nothing else could be heard there.

Aarya Ugrasen was gently patting the forehead of his wife but his eyes were lost in a gazing search…somewhere beyond the peaks of the wind.

When the child Kansa took his first breath in, after coming out of his mother's womb at that time, no lights were put up in Ugrasen's abode nor did the cymbals sound as a sign of festivity.... No one asked for sweets and neither did the residents of Mathura celebrate any festival. On the contrary on receiving the news of the birth of a son and the news of Pavanrekha becoming a mother…many eyebrows frowned in dissent. Those women who believed that the complete responsibility of protecting the chastity of women was theirs only twisted their mouths and contorted their lips. And Ugrasen...such a blackness was seen on his face that even a blind man could see it! That day the distressed Ugrasen quickly taking leave from the tasks of the ruling assembly had returned to his abode. No one was saying anything anywhere.

Ugrasen could be seen in Pavanrekha's room. Standing beside her couch for he first time he saw the face of the son.

He placed a gold coin in the tender hand of the child and slowly placed his hand on its forehead. Pavanrekha lay gazing at the act; her husband did not pick up the child and fondle it in his hands; in order to hide his face he turned it towards another direction. But how long can one remain like this also; when she turned her face again and looked at her husband, at that moment Ugrasen was wiping his eyes with the corner of his upper garment.

Holding the finger of his father Ugrasen, when the child Kansa placed his foot on the earth for the first time even at that time, the residents of Mathura ignored noticing this scene. It was as if…the finger of the ruler which was bearing the burden of the republic was not able to the burden of this child. Immediately, he handed over the child in the hands of his wife.

As he grew in age, Kansa could see that being the son of the ruler of the Republic Ugrasen, everyone in the township of Mathura was indeed showing him respect… but somehow or other the feeling of intimacy or the feeling of even an iota of love was missing...! Father Ugrasen also would not say anything special and it was this silence of his, which used to cause maximum pain to Kansa….

The youthful Kansa attained unprecedented skill in wrestling. The mace used to swing in his hand as if it was a flower in the hand. Youthfulness touching the sky with skills and mountain conquering capability and his powerful energy was desirous of breaking all bondages. Seeing this powerful form of Kansa, sometimes the residents of Mathura used to heave deep sighs…would whisper among themselves, "Whatever it be…this energetic son is after all not a Yadava...!" Sometimes someone would say this also, "Had only Kansa been a Yadava, the fortunes of the Vrajabhoomi would have scaled great heights…."

After the birth of Kansa, Pavanrekha hardly ever got out of the abode. This self-imposed solitude of his mother had become a fearsome puzzle for Kansa. Ugrasen also, if at all he would be present in any republican festival or in any community program would not sit with Pavanrekha in the assembly hall.

The festivals in which entire Mathura would be overflowing crowds, why does Pavanrekha remain deprived? Why? Why do not all these townsmen and the entire Yadava family behave with natural intimacy with Kansa? Why does father Ugrasen keep her thus far away? What is the reason for such a neglected state of Pavanrekha and for this solitude living? How many questions were cropping up? Kansa's lips got distorted. The muscles of his arms became tense. He clenched his fists tightly.

Father and mother...this life's most natural union also was appearing un-natural in front of Kansa and thus surrounded by them…he was also being steered towards an un-natural state of mind and a harsh resolve kept on binding him.... He will search out the forces which are pushing his mother towards this solitude living and when he finds out about them, he will destroy them; he would one day make these townsmen, this Yadava clan and every one else who are keeping her deprived of natural intimacy…fall at his feet.

And Narada arrived, becoming the instrument for fulfilling this resolve! the universal wandering ascetic arriving in Mathura, acknowledged the hospitality of the Vrajabhoomi.

"May well-being be with you, Son!" Narada blessed him thus, "Hope mother Pavanrekha is composed Son?"

Kansa looked here and there. Father Ugrasen and other esteemed personages stood far away. He got an unexpected privacy. "Devarshi did not enquire about the well-being of mother Pavanrekha from father Ugrasen; why did he ask me only?" This was yet another twist to his confusion?

"O Devarshi, mother has indeed been outcast...but my question is how long will she keep bearing this misery of aloneness?"

"Unknowingly, the mistake that has taken place at the hands of this unfortunate woman by acting against the dignity of the Vrajabhoomi...contrary to the chastity devotion...she has no other alternative than to bear this repentance form life till the end of her life span, Son!", said Narada, drawing in a deep breath.

"Devarshi!" Kansa went and sat at Narada's feet and said, "Kindly tell me for which sin is my mother enduring this punishment? Why this non-recognition towards me by this Yadava family of Mathura? O Bhagavan, please tell me...."

"Become composed Son!" said Narada placing his hand on Kansa's forehead, "The story of your birth and death which destiny has pre-determined for you, is something like this."

And Narada narrated that entire painful story. Kansa is the outcome of Durmil's sinful conduct; let not Ugrasen ever forget this, let not these Yadavas of the Vrajabhoomi forget this! Everyone accepted Kansa's arrival but there was no welcome attitude in that there was only helplessness.... His body began to burn like a hot copper vessel fire blazed forth in every cell of his body.

"And Son!" said Narada completing his narration, "Now listen to the story of your wound also. Deceived by the trick of Durmil's cunningness when your mother Pavanrekha came to know about his truth then her chastity exploded." On the other hand, satisfied by the successful attainment of another's wife, Durmil told Pavanrekha, 'O Sundari! As a result of our union a powerful son will be born out of your womb,' hearing this your mother became mad with rage. She herself was burning within and wished to burn even him who was associated with her miserable state. She said, "O wicked soul! Whatever is your portion who will be born from your this lowly act will be destroyed by a powerful and capable Yadava manifest in our lineage.... The Yadava clan will never tolerate the result of your impurity!"

Even as Narada was completing his narration, extreme anger and an emotion of insult arose in the mind of Kansa towards his father and the entire Republic and its townsmen. Instantaneously, he made a decision—None among the Republic, these townsmen, this entire Yadava family or even this Ugrasen had the right to outcast Pavanrekha never ever had…Kansa will crush all of them with the power of his arms—and because of the resentment of his mother he will change even the prophecy of his predicted death.

"However, I could not change the prophecy of death, O Krishna!" Since lot of blood had drained away, even the smile of the near to death Kansa's face had become faded. It appeared as if a weak ray had sprung up from the light of a solar eclipse covered sun.

Krishna was listening to all this; it was as if one by one some closed book's pages were being opened; he was listening and his face went on becoming full of compassion—Alas! Such an utter destruction of Kansa…. Suddenly, Krishna felt his victory over such an extremely powerful and most capable Kansa as hollow. Even before his birth, this man was the outcome of an insult meted out to a woman considered to be pure and stainless—and Krishna! even his very creation had also taken place at the same time and today he had also become the instrument for this unimaginable incident—The knowledge of the Truth of this matter made Krishna even more humble.

"Now you only tell me O Krishna!" Kansa's broken voice once again rose toward Krishna, that society which showed indifference towards an innocent woman despite having full trust in her chastity and that society, which outcast that woman, who had become the victim of deceit and cunningness…for her entire life span. What right has these spineless leaders of that society to rule? What offence had my mother done? Tell me, O Krishna! What offence had that boy Kansa done...who was born from her womb? Instead of destroying the wicked conduct Durmil, why did these cowards under the guise of traditional values and morality and in their own fire of hostility, commit innocent people to ashes?"

"Uncle!" said Krishna a very soft voice, "The justice and protection which an individual gets…this is indeed the strength of society, this is indeed the path of well-being; however after all, an individual is also part of society only isn't it? By offering society as a sacrificial oblation when can an individual become superior most and above all? In order to take revenge against a weak society you destroyed a Republic; you forcibly thrust your dictatorship over the Yadava clan."

"Republic! Which…which republic Krishna?" there was disrespect in Kansa's tone, that republic of an Ugrasen and a Vasudeva?" And then looking at Akroor he said, "and such an Akroor, who never ever thinks of leaving the happiness of authority…. Such a few in count leaders on whom a republic depends? In which all the common people are always engaged in shouting only victory cries! You… you…call this a Republic? Those who knew the truth did not have the courage to accept it. Accepting Pavanrekha as before, if the memory of the sorrowful chapter had been dissolved in the 'womb of forgetfulness' itself! then…O Krishna! this republic would have become immortal…and Kansa and Krishna both would have made it powerful…."

"No matter how great an individual is, Uncle…" Krishna tried to make him understand in a restrained tone, "even though the injustice that has occurred on an individual may be cruel even then, a powerful individual does not get the sanction to establish his authority! To struggle against injustice is a different matter...and making injustice an excuse, to usurp the entire society into one's own hand is another matter. This moment option is a far more cruel injustice, Uncle...an injustice should not be confronted through a higher injustice Uncle! How did you forget this basic truth?"

Kansa's eyes were turning inwards. Still remaining in the body a jerk was arising. Death had almost enveloped him.

"Truth is a mere imagination Krishna!" a deep gulf was arising out of Kansa's voice. His breath was getting stuck each and every word was drowned in pain, "some powerful people have always distorted this truth to suit their own convenience. There was a day when Aarya Ugrasen was truthful. Till today Maharaj Kansa was a supreme truth, in the coming morrow perhaps the cowherd Krishna of Gokul."

"No...please do not say so Uncle. Even more than Ugrasen, Kansa, and Krishna, a greater truth are all these people...." Krishna pointed towards the stone like gathered common men standing there.

The life breath of this motionless appearing gathering of men only, is the supreme truth. The one who is able to protect this truth and who is able to nourish its growth with maximum skill...that is the highest governance...an odd Kansa or Krishna cannot do this! Republicanism is great, Uncle...the greatest! You killed that Republic...."

"That Republic which killed an innocent Pavanrekha can never last, O Krishna...! That work which Kansa did, that work somewhere in the future could well be got done through the hands of Krishna also. If at all Pavanrekha's innocence is punished then...." Kansa could not talk further. His words got stuck.

Slowly, Krishna bent at the feet of Kansa. In his mind probably at that very moment a picture was painted—Getting freed from the imprisonment of Bhaumaasur, the picture of the women who got re-established in the mansions of Dwaraka—No...no! Now onwards another Pavanrekha will not be born....

"O Revered Sir Akroor!" Uddhav slowly woke up. Akroor who had lost himself in the past, "This fragrance obtained from watering the heavenly flowers, is vain now,

O Revered Sir! Did you not hear the gong striking the end of the third quarter of the night?"

"You had heard that sound of Krishna's conch Son?" It was as if Akroor was making a welcome speech. "Do you remember, Uddhav...killing that Bhaumaasur of Pragjyotishpur, Krishna had freed the thousands of women imprisoned in his inner private harem jail?"

"Yes, O Revered Sir, Not only had Krishna freed those women but he had re-established them among the most noble family women of Aaryavart.... After establishing them honourably in the Royal mansion of Dwaraka, he had given them equal status as Satyabhama and Rukimini."

"Had not such hundreds of innocent and sinless women been re-established...then...at the hands of Bhaumaasur... countless Kansas would have manifested out of that fire of injustice...O Uddhav...at that time...if Aaryavart had never accepted those women...the shadow of the injustice which had fallen upon one Pavanrekha would have then turned into ashes this Republic of the Vrajabhoomi for years together...and...if at all...Aaryavart had continued to do such similar cruel injustice towards hundreds of women...." Akroor got stuck up as he spoke.

"But at that time, the greatness of this act by Krishna and its value had not been appreciated...." Akroor said in a painful tone. "Krishna was not recognized in his Epoch, neither did we all also recognize that Epoch...when I am remembering today about my own sinful conduct also then...."

"O Revered Sir!" Uddhav could not say anything further.

Probably, some mammal was creating disorder in the flowing waters of Kalindi. Uddhav's voice got drowned in that sound.

□

16

"Uddhav" said Akroor as he kept gazing at the flow of the Kalindi with unwinking eyes, "Son, did you see this flow of Kalindi in fag end of night's dim light? See...now see...the form of Krishna in its blue waters! You are able to see, isn't it? The same peacock feather, same flute and there…see...Uddhav! see in that direction Uddhav!"

"Revered Sir..." Uddhav got stuck on that word itself….

"See there…Krishna and his dear cows and…in the midst of the flow, see that Govardhan mountain...it is as if Krishna has lifted it up with his little finger…it is as if Kalindi and Krishna have become one form..." as he was talking, Akroor became emotional.

"Revered Sir..." Uddhav halted his roving thoughts, "Kalindi is a great epoch.... On the shores of it…not only creation…but the expanse of the entire universe will be just a miniature. To dissolve into epoch in the form of a fraction of this universe…that…that is the path of knowledge, O Revered Sir! Be composed!"

"Composed!" Akroor began talking, "Perhaps today, as composed as I am now…that much I was never composed. That which was under the cover of a cowherd hidden that very thing has become picturesque today, Son.... In the assembly hall of Mathura that day Kansa was killed at the hands of Krishna but…but by some divine will if something contrary had occurred and…at the hands of Kansa." Akroors's throat choked.

"Please don't say so, O Revered Sir!"

"Let me speak Uddhav! Today let me say it all. I had got saved that day from becoming an instrument for Krishna's possible murder but…but even after being installed as the supreme personage of Aaryavart, I had placed him in the ordinary class of an ordinary thief...that sin returns to my memory and…and Uddhav, in order to make Mother Gandhaari's curse bear result I also will have to…."

"By recollecting the unfortunate past today, in this manner…" said Uddhav.

"Yes…today itself…today itself, Son! It is my wish that this unfortunate Akroor should not be able to see the first rays of the dawning sun. Now those sun's rays, the light of those rays cannot be borne by me. The attack which Kansa or Kaalayavan also could not make on Krishna, I had made such a life destroying attack…yes...I had done so. After committing the sin in the assembly hall of Mathura also, I only…."

"O Revered Akroor!"

"Yes, Son! That story of the Syamantak gem..." as he was speaking Akroor's head bent down.

"Aarya Satraajit..." addressing the assembly hall full of senior Yadavas one day, Krishna addressed the elderly Yadava armyman Satraajit thus, "by the grace of Lord Sun you have got such a rare gem which is indeed hard for the Deities...!"

Satraajit looked at Krishna startled; looked at the sun's rays shining over the prosperous domes of Dwaraka's mansions, looked at the shining gold-crowns of the Yadava heroes sitting in the assembly hall, cast his glance at the middle-aged Akroor and Vasudeva and at Saatyaki and Kritavarma seated a little far away! all were eager to hear the response of Satraajit to Krishna's saying.

"Krishna!" said Satraajit slowly, "That gem named Syamantak becoming delighted, Lord Sun had given me."

"This grace of Lord Sun is not a matter of pride only to Satraajit, but to the entire Yadava family, Revered Sir!"

said Krishna with delight, "That such an invaluable gem should be in Dwaraka, this fortune is for the entire Dwaraka township; we are all indeed blessed!"

"Krishna, whatever riches human beings have got till now, this wondrous gem is many times more valuable than them!" said Balaram and then facing Satyaajit, asked, "One has also heard that this wonderful gem gives you eight gold coins early morning in the form of sun's gift?"

"You have heard right, O Sankarshan!" said Satraajit, accepting it, "This gem is the source of limitless gold coins—and everyday early morning eight gold coins are obtained."

Everyone remained spell-bound with wonder. Krishna's sight was steadily gazing at the horizon beyond Dwaraka. After a short silence Krishna said, in a very solemn tone—

"Satraajit, in this achievement of yours, all the Yadavas and the residents of Dwaraka should become partners... what greater privilege than this could be there!"

Akroor's eyes met Satraajit's eyes. He knew about this eternal treasure of Satraajit but there was something else also pulling him towards Satraajit; Satraajit's daughter Satyabhama.... Incomparable grace, sandal-like complexion! She was Satraajit's one and only daughter. She had taken deep roots in Aarya Akroor's mind. The longing to get Satyabhama! adult Akroor was helpless in front of that longing.... And he had already placed his this wish in front of Satraajit.

"Satraajit!" Akroor had said, "To tie the knot of wedlock of a daughter like Satyabhama with Akroor, the commander-in-chief of the Yadava army.... What more could be more auspicious than that? By handing over Satyabhama to me, may you become freed from the worldly bondage of duty."

"Akroor!" Satraajit's voice was fully restrained, "I have already chosen Aarya Shatadhanva for Satyabhama in my mind. She will become only Shatadhanva's wife."

The status of Shatadhanva was hardly anything to speak of in the Yadava clan. Akroor was the commander-in-chief of the Yadava army. What if he was a little aged! Rejecting me in comparison with Shatadhanva? Bitterness towards Satraajit arose in Akroor's mind.

"O Devaki Nandan!" said Satraajit cautiously, "I am feeling blessed by the good wishes of the entire Yadava family and its worship worthy elders."

"Revered Sir!" said Krishna in a gentle tone, "That the prosperity arising from the attainment of the Syamantak should be useful for the entire community, that itself is the better option. Your greatness and the merit of the Yadava family lie in that."

Everyone's ears stood stiff. Satraajit's face fell a bit—A clever delight crept into Akroor's eyes.

"That Lakshmi…attained by one's efforts the ownership of that only, is considered personal Aarya! That Lakshmi obtained devoid of effort is meant for the community in this lies the path of welfare for everyone..." the ever familiar charming smile was blooming in Krishna's face.

"And therefore, not by virtue of being the owner of Syamantak…but as the faithful trusty of that it is desirable that its benefit should be availed by all the common people of Dwaraka, O Revered Satraajit!" Balaram supported Krishna.

"Vasudev Krishna!" Satraajit's voice was a bit raised, "I honour your thoughts but the Syamantak—that is the blessing of my God worshipped Lord Sun. It will remain with me; it will completely remain with me only."

"The earth, wind, water—If the individual has ownership only on the Lakshmi obtained from these three elements and that too by his own sincere efforts then it is in the welfare of society. But Aarya Satraajit, the final decision in this matter depends on your good wishes alone! The Yadava family will certainly not commit any transgression." There was the resounding of subtle authority in Krishna's voice.

"I cannot surrender this gracious gift of mine to the community.... Forgive me Keshav!" saying so Satraajit closed the matter.

Krishna did not insist more. There was strain on the face of Sankarshan Balaram. Akroor was disappointed. Yadava assembly dissolved.

Krishna had told in the full assembly that the Syamantak gem should be surrendered to the community for everybody's benefit by this utterance Satraajit had become worried and perturbed. Keeping silent, the manner in which the Yadava clan supported Krishna's suggestion.... Satraajit could sense only community envy in it. Fearing that Krishna should not get hold of the gem through some other means, Satraajit handed over the gem to his younger brother Prasena and kept this matter hidden from everybody.

But after a few days a bad incident occurred.

Some wild animal killed Prasena who had gone to the forest for hunting. At that time that Syamantak gem was adorning the neck of Prasena. The magnetic attraction of the red gem pulled the forester Jaambuvaan towards it. He removed the gem from Prasena's neck. But he did not have any knowledge about its value. Thinking it to be some attractive piece of stone, he gave it his small child to play.

When Satraajit heard the news about the killing of Prasena and the Syamantak gem's disappearance, he poured out his entire anger on all the Yadavas—

"O Yadavas...it was just some time back that Krishna had demanded that gem from me; this all of you are already aware. I did not accept that unjust demand and that is why Krishna has resorted to this mean path and taken custody of the gem. Krishna and Balaram, who are advocating the prosperity of the community in reality, wished for the ownership of this wonderful gem now nothing remains hidden."

A few elderly Yadavas began feeling that Satraajit's doubt was true. An argument ensued. If at all a wild animal had killed Prasena then how can the gem from his neck disappear? If Krishna himself resorts to such a deed, then where is the dignity of the Yadava family?

The news reached Krishna's ears. Once again his world alluring smile became prominent. He decided to search for the Syamantak gem. He carefully examined the spot where Prasenajit was killed. Apart from the foot-prints of the wild animal, there were footsteps of Jaambuvaan also. On the basis of this finding, he searched out Jaambuvaan's house. It seemed as if the radiant rays of the Syamantak itself, which had spread even far away from Jaambuvaan's house was showing Krishna, Jaambuvaan's house. Krishna reached there.

In the beginning, Jaambuvaan refused to return the gem. As it is, he had no value for Syamantak but if some townsman comes and challenges his rule, how can he bear that? He decided to fight with Krishna.

But where did Jaambuvaan have even an inkling of whom he was thinking of fighting with? As soon as he became aware about this, he left the thought of fighting. As it is for him the gem was equal to mud. He extended his hand of friendship towards Krishna. Krishna accepted his friendship.

"Krishna!" said Jaambuvaan with humility, "By accepting my friendship you have obliged me. You have come to my house for the first time. What gift shall I give you? By accepting the hand of my daughter Jaambuvati, may you make our friendship long lasting."

Krishna accepted Jaambuvaan's proposal.

Krishna returned to Dwaraka along with his wife Jaambuvati and the Syamantak gem.

The very next day that gem was placed in front of everyone in the assembly—"Here is your wonderful gem. The witness to its recovery is my wife Jaambuvati and my forester friend Jaambuvaan, who is now my father-in-law. If among any of the Yadava leaders, there is doubt regarding

Satraajit's allegation then it is essential to have such doubts proved as baseless."

"Please forgive me Krishna!" said an ashamed Satraajit, "the allegation made by me was a result of my resentment and my lamentation, O Madhusoodan! Please forget it with a large heart that is my sincere prayer!"

"O Revered Sir, this gem is yours. Please keep it with you itself."

"O Keshav!" said Satraajit became emotional, "I had lost this gem. You only have retrieved it. Now you yourself keep it!"

"Not at least at this hour." said Krishna, "If at all I accept it now then again a doubt may creep in, that even in searching this out I had some gain to get from it. Hence you are only the real owner of this, O Revered Sir! Please keep Lord Sun's gracious gift with yourself only."

Satraajit was left overwhelmed. The Yadav assembly kept looking at Krishna and Satraajit with a deep reverence. It was only in Akroor's eyes that unhappiness was glowing. He was unable to forget his insult till now. His enmity towards Satraajit became more deep rooted.

"Krishna!" said Satraajit gratefully, "If at all you are returning the Syamantak gem to me then please accept my gem like daughter Satyabhama and provide me a small opportunity to become relieved from my indebtedness. This is my humble prayer."

Becoming delighted, the entire Yadava assembly raised victory cries. A smile spread over Krishna's face—that smile had expressed assent.

Akroor looked towards Shatadhanva sitting in a corner of the assembly. All four eyes were throwing sparks of fire towards Satraajit.

□

17

All this was unbearable to Akroor. Not only was the gem found but Krishna returned it also to Satraajit and a grateful Satraajit gave his daughter Satyabhama in marriage to Krishna; how did all this unimaginable occur all together at once? And what was the counter answer to this?

After a few days, meeting Shatadhanva alone, Akroor had a talk with him, "Shatadhanva!" said Akroor cautiously, "That you should take Satyabhama's hands in wedlock was Aarya Satraajit's desire. You know it isn't it?"

"No, I did not know so. Yes, I had certainly expressed my desire to marry Satyabhama in front of Satraajit", said Shatadhanva.

"Then what did Satraajit say to it?"

"He had not show any special disposition. I had thought that if ever I get an opportunity later I shall repeat my request."

Akroor fell into a quandary. Satraajit had told him that he had in his mind Shatadhanva's name and Shatadhanva did not even know about it. Then had Satraajit said it merely to keep Akroor at a distance? Akroor's anger increased further.

"Now give up such a hope, Son", said Akroor gently provoking him, "Satyabhama has become unattainable to you. But...."

"But what Revered Sir?"

"However, the reason due to which Satraajit's ego is scaling the skies, if that Syamantak gem does not remain with him and if he becomes deprived of it then his conceit will be shattered."

"But how is this possible? To displace the Syamantak gem from him is not possible.... Shatadhanva's eyebrows tensed, I have a lot of hostility in my mind towards Satraajit, Aarya Akroor!"

"Then why should not that gem be with Shatadhanva?" And as if weaving some secret in Shatadhanva's ears he said thus, "My dear, Satraajit is an old man and you are a young man! Can you not find a way for Saraajit? Finish him off."

Shatadhanva got startled, "Killing of Satraajit? O Revered Sir!" Then he controlled himself, "As it is this task is easy Revered Sir.... But...if the entire Yadavas and Krishna himself search out that killer...."

"You are unnecessarily getting frightened Shatadhanva!" Akroor began to make him understand, "If at all such a problem arises I shall help you. Once Satraajit is killed and you get the ownership of the gem."

Shatadhanva came under the sway of Akroor's words. The enmity which was brewing in the minds of both now joined together. Gaining the support of a senior respectable Yadav like Akroor, Shatadhanva's uncovered fire of enmity blazed forth. He decided to kill Satrajit. If not Satyabhama at least I shall get the Syamantak. Satraajit must be taught a lesson. Both started looking out for an opportune moment.

And that favorable opportunity arrived very soon.

As the news that the five Pandavas along with mother Kunti were burnt to ashes in the wax house spread, Krishna, Balaram and everyone else got shaken up. At this hour one should be present in Hastinapur to console Grandsire Bheeshma and Dhritarashtra and with this in mind, both along with senior Yadavas proceeded to Hastinapur. All of a sudden the task of looking after Dwaraka fell into the hands of Akroor. Shatadhanva got his heart wished opportunity. Not only was he getting the opportunity to make a plan for the task and to carry it out, he was also getting shield of

Akroor who was to govern Dwarka in absence of Krishna and Balaram. He did that which was objectionable—the killing of Satraajit and stealing of the Syamantak gem. There was great commotion in Dwaraka and also whispering voices could be heard. It was opined that this task was done before the eyes of Akroor and that there was the hand of Shatadhanva also in it; doubts were being expressed but Akroor did not pay any attention towards that matter at all. But how can it remain unranked after the return of Krishna?

Krishna called Shatadhanva. Balaram was extremely angry at the robbery of the invaluable gem. He decided that by hook or by crook the gem has got to be retrieved. Krishna was calm. Before blaming Shatadhanva, he wished to hear about the entire matter from the mouth of Shatadhanva itself.

Krishna's call—Shatadhanva's guilty conscious started shivering. His steps were full of fear. To confront Krishna in the packed assembly it was impossible! The suspicious views of the Yadavas and the presence of Krishna. Now let alone the matter about the Syamantak the question of saving himself cropped up. He ran to Akroor.

"Aarya Akroor, the protection of the Syamantak is a far-fetched question now, how can my life be saved? Now... now...you...only you can help me."

"Shatadhanva!" saying so, Akroor remained silent. The circumstances was serious because Krishna Balaram were in front. That it was difficult to face them, who else than Akroor knew better! By the killing of Satraajit, the fire of enmity within him had indeed been appeased now it would be wise to pull his neck out of this and in the bargain, if he can also get custody of the Syammantak gem nothing like it. After all, Shatadhanva is not worthy of the Syamantak also.

The crooked intellect of the bold Akroor started making calculated moves. That the Syamantak gem should be with him and that everyone should acknowledge Shatadhanva as guilty and that Krishna's anger be appeased—thus leaving no trace of doubt remain in anyone's mind and that everything would pass off from the minds of others' heads smoothly.

"Shatadhanva!" said Akroor with great caution, "Krishna should not be left with any doubt for that, you should leave Dwaraka and go far away."

"But...but Aarya...how can I bear the burden of taking care of the Syamantak? If you consent to take care of the gem then I shall run away somewhere far."

That's it! This was exactly what Akroor wanted... Shatadhanva said exactly what was in his mind. He hid the Syamantak like some secret treasure. Shatadhanva was not to be seen anywhere there...he left Dwaraka and ran far away.

That Shatadhanva ran away—hearing the news Balaram began trembling with rage. He roared—"Krishna, we cannot leave the sinner Shatadhanva alive any more. Come, let us follow him, we have to recover the Syamantak."

All the Yadavas approved what Balaram said.

"The recovery of the Syamantak gem is momentary, Krishna", said the senior Yadavas, "If the Yadava family begins to resort to killing for the sake of material benefits then this rule will become scattered and destroyed. It is imperative that Shatadhanva should be officially punished by the governing body."

Krishna nodded his head in agreement.

After all where will Shatadhnva go. He was running to save his life into villages townships, mountains and in the jungles. And it was then that he came to know that Krishna Balaram were following him to catch him and pronounce death penalty on him. Now even to run and hide himself somewhere became difficult. His legs refused to move. Sometimes within a cave or sometimes amidst the branches of some tree top. His chariot and horses had long deserted him, now even his legs were not co-operating.

Shatadhanva's horse and chariot? Krishna stopped on the path itself.

"Elder Brother!" he told Balaram, "Shatadhanva is running on foot somewhere on this path. It is not justice to catch the culprit with the help of chariot and horses. We should also abandon the chariot and horses."

"Janardan...your views are lawful but...to abandon this chariot and horses unsafe in this unknown territory and go on foot? If some one takes them away?"

"In that case, Brother!" Krishna opined, "You halt among the people nearby and protect them. I shall catch Shatadhanva immediately."

Balaram also did accordingly. Krishna moved forward on the mountainous path.

Not very far off, he found the footprints of Shatadhanva. This was the final lap. If at all Krishna catches him, he will not spare him hence to confront him was the one and only way. The exhausted Shatadhanva decided to confront Krishna in a last contest, wagering his life and both came in front of each other. There was fear in Shatadhanva's eyes and compassion in Krishna's eyes; the same world alluring smile was playing on his lips. Shatadhanva could sense his final moments approaching. He closed his eyes, what was inevitable did not occur. The arrow which had risen to give the death punishment stopped for a moment… why? Krishna felt a bit uneasy then he let the arrow perform its action.

Shatadhanva's head got severed and got separated from the trunk. The tired body which had been running attained permanent peace. Krishna slowly went near him. Plucking a flower from a nearby tree, he placed it near the feet of Shatadhanva; he kept a basil leaf in his mouth and after circumambulating his body he saluted it. Bringing water from a nearby flowing stream, he bestowed peace to his five elements.

The guilty was punished but…the gem? That could not to be seen. Krishna felt uneasy.

"Brother," returning Krishna narrated the entire news to Balaram, "The guilty got punishment but the gem was not found, it was not with him."

"How can this be?" Balaram got surprised, "Shatadhanva was indeed the thief! The gem must certainly be with him only."

"But it was not there!" said Krishna, "The killing of Satraajit was done by Shatadhanva; this truth is indisputable."

"And he had taken the Syamantak gem; this is also indisputable Krishna."

"Yes, this is also indisputable", said Krishna, "but the gem was not there with him now; this is also indisputable."

"Krishna!" said Balaram in a deep voice, "If the Syamantak gem was not with Shatadhanva, then he would not run away this way like a thief.... When we summoned him to the Yadava assembly then instead of presenting himself why did he have to thus run away?"

"Brother!" said Krishna, "All these questions are perplexing me too."

Balaram fell into deep thought. The Syamantak gem was priceless. Krishna also had an eye on it. He only, had raised the topic of its utility for the benefit of everyone. Balaram felt uneasy; hope Krishna did not have a desire to embezzle that gem? Hope it is not so that after killing Shatadhanva, Krishna took it in his hands? And…that he may not have to give a portion of the wealth from this priceless gem to Balaram! and hence he hid it away somewhere. Is it the wish of Krishna to keep Balaram and the entire Yadava clan in darkness?

"What are you thinking, Brother?" asked Krishna with a simple attitude, "Come now, let us go to Dwaraka and narrate the whole news to the elders."

"Krishna!" said Balaram suddenly, "the gem to bring which we had proceeded without getting it or without obtaining any indication about it; it does not behove of us to return to Dwaraka!"

"Brother!" said Krishna again with great ease, "We had proceeded to punish the guilty! That we have done, the matter of getting the gem is momentary isn't it?"

"I am unable to trust your words, Krishna!" said Balaram clearly this time, "I am not so innocent as to get trapped in the snare of your words."

"Meaning? What is this you are saying, Brother?" Krishna was startled. The peacock feather from his forehead slipped down. The usually simple smile which would be playing on his lips, disappeared, and his lips were quivering.

Balaram's anger was not controllable within any limits now—"It is certain that you have got the Syamantak gem from Shatadhanva but out of greed…that you should not have to give me a share from it; such deceit came into your mind…and you hid it somewhere!"

"Brother…brother...!" Krishna broke down. Such distress had never ever been heard in his voice. For the first time in life, he was surrounded by helplessness!

"Until I get information about the Syamantak I shall not return to Dwaraka. I shall not come to narrate such a shameful story to the Yadavas of Dwaraka; I cannot do so…."

"Brother, you are doing injustice...."

"The verdict of justice injustice, will be done by time." Balaram was firm on his decision, "I shall go to Mithila from here and remain there; I shall search for the Syamantak gem and until you admit your bad act; till then I shall not step into Dwaraka. Convey my respects to all the Yadava heroes, Krishna…." And Sankarshan turned on his back.

□

18

Krishna's sight settled on elder brother Balaram's back. "Brother!" he again called out but this time merely his lips uttered, sound did not come out. What Balaram had said, that was completely beyond imagination. The Syamantak...when Krishna had raised its topic at that time, his vision was not limited to the Yadava clan alone—not even to the citizens of Dwaraka—not even on Aaryavart which was bound within limits—his vision had settled on the entire future.... On the well-being of those generations, which had not even born was in his mind; how can Krishna ever look at such a Syamantak which had extra-terrestrial powers with such a narrow vision!

And now Balaram was saying, "Krishna! that which Satraajit did, what Shatadhanva did, you did an even more lowly act than that, O Janardan...Krishna, you are a thief...thief...."

Darkness spread across the sky, the waves in the water sources stopped quivering, the flowing wind hid behind the leaves of the trees, the cooing of the birds got choked...the peacock feather bent its head.

Krishna kept on looking at Balaram's back till it disappeared from sight.

All the shadows of the incidents hiding somewhere in a corner of his mind, began surfacing up—how easy it had been for him to install Ugrasen as the head of the Republic after killing Kansa. Kansa's killing was easy; conquering Jarasandh was also not a burden, there was not even a moment's hesitation in fighting with Kaalayavan. But

Balaram? how to retort your allegations, how to encounter you? You! you...are my brother, father Vasudeva's blood... Krishna stood for a moment like a statue and the very next moment closed his eyes.

When he opened his eyes again, everything was as it was before—the sky was filled with light, the waters of the water sources started dancing, the wind was fondling the leaves and the cooing of the birds was piercing the atmosphere.

The seed of some tomorrow, which was to germinate in future had been sown. A sound emanated from amidst the leaves, as if waiting to be uttered on the Kurukshetra field—

"Na me karmaani limpanti, na karmaphale sprihaa"... (न में कर्माणि लिम्पन्ति, न कर्मफले स्पृहा)... (Actions do not taint Me, nor have I a desire for the fruits of actions.)

The manner in which Balaram had renounced Dwaraka, all the Yadavas were grieved at that. Krishna consoled everyone and decided to find the whereabouts of the Syamantak gem. But the seed of doubt which Balaram had sown, had made its way into many minds. No one was revealing it—but Krishna could clearly see the distrust playing in everyone's eyes.

If the Syamantak was not retrieved, the future of Dwaraka cannot remain strong. Hiding this pain in the depth of his mind, Krishna was smiling his normal smile with ease. Today Balaram said it, tomorrow everyone will start saying it. Then what Shatadhanva did, that itself everyone will follow; mutual distrust, lack of faith and ultimately it would turn out into a frightful hour.

Along with other Yadavas, Akroor also was expressing his pain over whatever had happened, by which no one should have doubt on him. With the gold-coins obtained from the Syamantak his treasury was getting filled up.

He knew one thing that even this limitless flow of wealth was in the end perishable. Therefore, its use should point to the path of the higher worlds. Akroor opened the doors of his treasury. Yajnas began in his mansion. One after the other, the fire of Mahayajnas kept burning uninterruptedly. Apart from the echoes of "Swaaha", Dwaraka was filled with the fragrance of the flowing ghee. That Akroor's mansion should be filled, not only in Dwaraka but…it should become the focal point of the entire region…that was the manner in which Brahmins, austere rishis, and begging mendicants were flocking the mansion.

For days, months, years, these Yajnas were going on and this itself alerted Krishna—From where did so much wealth come into Akroor's treasury? How was Akroor alone able to spend so much wealth which even the entire Vrishni clan could not spend!

Other than the Syamantak no other power could give so much wealth. Krishna was startled at first and now he made the decision.

"O Revered Akroor!", focusing his eyes on Akroor who was sitting in the assembly Krishna said with gravity, "The Syamantak gem…."

The happiness which had been blooming on Akroor's face from the charity and punya which he had been doing, suddenly disappeared within a fraction of a moment. Compassion manifested out of Krishna's smile.

"Just as Satraajit and Shatadhanva have become merely a name of the past that path cannot become the path of the Revered Akroor", said Krishna, "The Yadava army commander-in-chief Akroor has become absorbed in penance."

"Krishna!" Akroor could not say anything further. His heart began shrieking.

"Yes, O Revered Sir!" said Krishna, "You are not Shatadhanva, indeed you are a seer of the future in the depths of the sky. That the Syamantak gem should be swallowed up by the future's-morrow and that by bad luck, if the Revered Akroor should become its instrument. Then, it will give maximum pain to Krishna…." Krishna's tone became moist and he perplexed the entire assembly.

"After completing the journey of this world, the Revered Akroor will become united with the Deities." Krishna went on talking, "whatever is visible...seeing beyond that what great value of wealth also attaches on those people, those who make this world also blessed."

"Krishna...Krishna..." Akroor could not bear it any longer, he got up and stood. He was shaken up from within. Krishna was indeed speaking the truth. After performing so many countless Yajnas also, the final goal is after all to become united with the universal soul. In comparison with that union the begetting of this Syamantak, is after all.

Removing the gem which always used to be fixed on his limbs, Akroor kept it in front of the assembly and without saying anything bent his head. The Yadava assembly remained spell-bound.

A messenger was sent to bring back the displeased Balaram who was residing in Milthila, to Dwaraka.

While returning to Dwaraka many emotions were arising in Balaram's mind. He was getting terribly angry on Akroor and he also was ashamed beyond limits.

"Brother!" said Krishna, bowing his head at Balaram's feet, "Dwaraka has once again got back its light, I am so delighted about it today!"

"May there be well-being, brother!" Balaram felt embarrassed. As if nothing had happened, Krishna told Balaram about well-being of father Vasudeva and mother Devaki. The entire Yadava family kept chatting.

The next day Krishna produced the Syamantak gem in front of the Yadava assembly. Balaram's sight got fixed on the gem and all eyes were on Balaram. Krishna's eyes were not on the Yadava assembly nor on Balaram and neither on the gem. His sight was fixed on Akroor's dampened face.

Balaram was getting restless to get control over the gem but with great effort was maintaining restraint. He had indeed been proved guilty in the eyes of the Yadavas and especially in Krishna's eyes.

"Brother" said Krishna, "this gracious gift of Lord Sun is really incomparable."

"But till now only Satraajit, Shatadhanva and Akroorji have taken its benefit" said Balaram. His greed for getting the gem was now not getting hidden even though he was attempting to hide it.

For the first time Krishna looked at Balaram. He recognized the greed shining in his eyes.

"Don't say so, Brother!" said Krishna, "The Revered Akroor used the wealth obtained from the Syamantak for the welfare of the entire creation. Yajna is after all the principle meant for upholding creation."

Some Yadavas nodded their heads in agreement. For the first time there was slight composure beaming on Akroor's face.

"Brother!" said Krishna, "There is no dearth of wealth with the Yadavas. And just a little wealth or gold-coins...."

"Some!" Balaram's eyes opened widely, "The never exhausting Syamantak is the source of limitless wealth Brother...."

"That wealth which can be counted, that wealth which can be measured, how can that be said to be limitless and unbounded? If at all there is anything which is limitless and unbounded then it has become the faith in the Yadavas, their unbroken chain of trust. Sacrificing this attitude it is not wise to count some gold-coins..." said Krishna.

"Krishna! You only had said, that the wealth obtained through the Syamantak is devoid of effort. The source of effortless wealth cannot be for an individual but only for the collectivity."

"This gem is eternal for the prosperity of the collectivity Brother", Krishna said emphatically, "But the prosperity of the collectivity cannot stand on the foundation without faith. Have you forgotten the history of this gem?"

Balaram was startled. What is Krishna trying to hint at, by talking about the history of the gem? He on account of the gem, he had pronounced Krishna as a guilty person.... Considering Krishna as a thief he had insulted him. All the Yadavas had looked at Krishna with suspicious eyes, thinking Krishna to be thief and all this occurred on account of this gem.

"This gem belongs to Akroorji, Brother! Akroor welded the chain of broken trust once again. The value of this chain cannot be estimated. This gem is safe in the hands of Akroor who has been giving such unheard of charity and the pride of everyone is in this only..." there was a sense of assertion in Krishna's tone.

Balaram could not give any counter argument now. The mind of the Yadavas, which had become stained by the gem now became free from anxiety; a fury got pacified. In place of excitement, a decisive conclusion prevailed now.

For Akroor, this blessing of Krishna was beyond imagination. Even after knowing the intensity of Balaram's greed, the manner in which Krishna had turned the whole matter by that, he became emotional. They certainly were sitting together but his head was looking down out of shame. That he had a hand in Satraajit's killing, this everyone indeed knew by now. If only Krishna had not rescued him then all the Yadavas; especially Balaram would have for his bad act...and if at all that had happened then he....

It was the evening of the same day. It was a corner of Krishna's mansion. Two persons were sitting alone—Krishna and Akroor.

"Krishna!" Akroor's throat choked, and his eyes became moist, "Your touch has given even my bad act the form of justice; this compassion of yours is a hundred times more valuable than the Syamantak O Keshav!"

"O Ravered Sir!" Krishna wiped the eyes of Akroor. Akroor thought—Oh my God! The finger on which the Sudarshan Chakra spins like a flower, how tender those fingers are! "The conduct of injustice is performed by the body. The moment the mind is able to convince the body of its mistake that moment indeed, becomes unforgettable. You made that moment come true so easily, O Keshav!

"Krishna...O Krishna...forgive me!", wailed Akroor, "You only had said—To merge into the abode of the universal gods, this is the final goal. Please help me, Krishna! May my journey proceed towards the attainment of these universal gods. You only have to steer me towards that destination."

The ocean of grace welled up in Krishna's eyes. Akroor got completely drenched in the ocean of that peacock feather and...Krishna embraced him.

The next day Akroor's chariot was moving forward on the path towards Mathura. He could not meet the eyes of the people of Dwaraka. At the time of this parting Akroor had no idea that Krishna's eyes were still looking at the dust raised by trot of his chariot's horses from far-off dispersing his compassionate smile.

The night had not yet faded in the garden of Akroor. Along with Uddhav, as they sank into the years old memories of past and thus sinking, they went on sinking. Uddhav thought...at times, do memories also turn into a curse? And, is forgetfulness a great boon? Hope Akroor is not influenced by this curse....

"Uddhav!" said Akroor as if he was touching with his hands the cool breeze coming sifted through the Tamaal tress, "To have a bath in the Yamuna river on such a lovely morning...a epoch has passed. Now this body which has held fast old age in its fists, cannot relish this joy also.... Come, Son...Let me purify my body in the waters of this Kalindi."

"Revered Sir!" said Uddhav feeling somewhat embarrassed, "Now please do not give trouble to the body, take rest for a little while."

"Rest?" Akroor's burdensome voice arose from somewhere within, "Yes, now the body has to be given rest. But not momentarily but permanently."

Uddhav supported Akroor. Keeping his hand on Uddhav's shoulder, Akroor came out. The early morning hours, seeing these two going towards the Kalindi remained wonder struck. There was peace in the mansion now.

Very slowly they proceeded on the royal path of Mathura; leaving behind feeble footprints in the dust.

"Uddhav!" suddenly Akroor said, "Are you seeing these footprints imprinted in the dust? At some time Krishna's footprints must also have been imprinted in the same dust!"

"Yes, Revered Sir!" said Uddhav, "today at this hour, our footprints have been imprinted in this dust within an hour, other countless footprints will become prominent in this; what difference does it make to the earth, whether it is a man or an animal.... It holds everyone with equanimity in its lap. Even before Krishna, who knows? how many footprints must have been imprinted in this earth!

"And yet no footprint became eternal, Uddhav!"

"Eternity?" Udhhav said, "Perhaps eternity is a curse, Revered Sir! Let it not be said to be a boon; may it be said that Nature is free from that curse."

Akroor suddenly became serious. Until they came and stopped at the banks of the expansive Kalindi, he did not say anything. The flow of the Yamuna was coming out of the blanket of darkness. Here and there on the banks, tortoises were lying like stone-statues. Deep somewhere three four cows were getting out of their night laziness. This silence was as if it was wishing to say something. On the same banks, a peacock standing under a fig-tree suddenly raised its neck and began cooing; then he fluttered his wings...and then folded his wings and a single feather got separated from it and fell on the earth.

Akroor stopped hesitantly, he went near that peacock, the peacock did not run away from there. Uddhav was wonder struck. With great difficulty Akroor bent and picked up that feather. The peacock again cooed, a smile spread over Akroor's face and said with a beaming face, "Uddhav...! Now why can't each an every peacock feather become Krishna? Why can't Krishna be found in each and every water drop of the Kalindi? Tell me O Son, tell me…Krishna must have touched this air of the Vrindavan sometime or other and Krishna's footprints must also be imprinted in this earth somewhere or other." Akroor continued speaking under the sway of emotions.

"Revered Sir, Akroor!" said Uddhav slowly; then he had strayed somewhere else.

"And...and…you did see the eyes of that cow Uddhav? Did you hear the tingling of the bell around his neck? Did you see the light lines arising in the leaves of that tree? There was the beautiful form of child Krishna in them!"

"Revered Sir, O Revered Sir! Please become composed; the auspicious moment of early dawn is passing away. The flow of Kalindi is awaiting us; come let us take bath…" Uddhav was waking up Akroor from his emotional state.

Now the flow was right in front. The smoke arising from some far-off worship place was making strange shapes in the sky. No sooner the legs touched the water then the water rings began running fast; there was some stirring among some tortoises; some fishes began running.

Akroor stood in waist high water filling his palms with water he offered oblations in the direction of east and then suddenly turned towards Uddhav. He was standing a little far away and offering oblations towards the east. "Uddhav! Vasudeva was my friend and of the same age; but I did not get the good fortune like him!"

"What good fortune, Revered Sir? That of becoming Krishna's father?"

"No, Krishna was Vasudeva's son that is just the result of fate. He belonged to the entire creation Uddhav!"

"So?"

"From the universe devoid of Krishna, Vasudeva was able to get liberation. He held up his breath; he dissolved into Yoga contemplation. He continued his journey in the direction in which Krishna's footprints were imprinted; what Vasudeva could do, Akroor could not do…" he was speaking with such indifference as if he were speaking about someone else.

"The path of liberation is laid down in different ways for everyone; it is not as if the Revered Akroor is unaware of it", said Uddhav spreading out his hand in the water, "The liberation of each body is the result of his deeds committed by him in the past."

"You have said the truth Son!" said Akroor, "My those deeds will not permit me to attain liberation by the path of Yoga contemplation. The suffering which I gave Krishna, he did not allow even a small portion of that suffering to touch me...he gave me the merit of conducting Yajnas; stitching the guilt of robbery to my lips, he accepted it himself…." Two tears dropped flowing out from Akroor's eyes suddenly brought about flood in the Yamuna. The water which was touching the waist now reached up to the chest; the cool flow suddenly became warm.

Many cows standing on the banks began bellowing.

"See…see Uddhav...see there, focus your eyes on that big ring there above the flow…" Akroor drew the attention of Uddhav, "Over the surface of that deep water, it appears as if the wind is drawing a shape in Kalindi are you able to see that shape Brother?"

Uddhav kept looking with steady eyes. Akroor was now standing in chest deep waters. Water was dripping from his long hairs. Those rings pointed out by Akroor!

Uddhav became spellbound.

What is it that he had seen?

"This is the abode of the universal god Uddhav!" said Akroor.

A unique shape was rising up in the deep flow of the waters.

"I did not get the fortune of Yoga contemplation Uddhav!" Akroor blabbered, "Now please see…the universal god himself has descended into the flow of Kalindi. Now bid me farewell Son! Krishna had said—'Your place of residence will be among the universal god'…. That moment has arrived! The fortune of begetting self-immolation in the waters of Kalindi!"

Uddhav trembled. He had never had such intense goose-bumps ever before. He had not experienced such coolness even while he had performed the morning salutations standing in the ice-cold waters of the Himalayan waters of Alaknanda, while going through the schedule of his pilgrimage. Uddhav had bathed in the flow of the waters of Kalindi countless times. He was familiar with each and every drop of this flow but today? this moment? the shape which was rising up in the waters of Kalindi, he had never seen such a scene ever before. Hope this is not the description of That, which Sanjay had narrated to Dhritarashtra, hope this is itself not That Vision of universal form-divine manifestation? Uddhav started looking with wide open eyes—his ears stood up on ends.

One…with many faces…many eyes…One, with many wonderful visual optics…One, with many divine ornaments…One, with many weapons…adorned with divine necklace and attire…smeared with divine fragrance… radiant…like the brilliance of thousands of suns descended from the endless pure skies. Uddhav's eyes remained unmoving….

Is this the divine manifestation? Is this? Is this…the abode of the universal god?

"Akroor! Your place of residence will be among the universal god…" Is this the moment which Krishna had talked of? Has that moment arrived?

"May you prosper Son!" saying so Akroor moved forward slowly, "Before the shape which has descended on the big rings disappears before that itself may the truth of Krishna's words...."

Uddhav could not utter anything.

"And after all Akroor is also a Yadava only, isn't it Uddhav?" said Akroor. Now his body was in shoulder deep waters, "As long as I am alive how can Mother Gandhari's words fructify?"

Uddhav's memory was as if struck by lightning—Akroor was speaking the truth. Mother Gandhari had cursed the Vrishni clan with total destruction. Along with Krishna Balaram the entire Yadava clan had dissolved in the Prabhas field. Now only Akroor was remaining. As long as Akroor's five elemental body does not get absorbed in the vastness, the destruction of the Vrishni clan will remain incomplete.

"Just as Arjuna bid had farewell to father Vasudeva in the same manner, Son you also...offer here, sacrificial oblations but for the welfare of everyone Brother!" said Akroor.

There was commotion in Uddhav's mind, "Why am I unable to stop Akroor? Why is the renunciation of this extremely decrepit body by Akroor not disturbing his mind? Why is a supremely peaceful feeling arising in his mind that this renunciation of the body is indeed lawful.

Uddhav began looking at the rings being manifested in front.

Just as gathering the sky, earth and Rudra, Marut, Aditya, and all the accomplished pervading all the directions—just as the flow of all rivers flow towards the ocean, in the same manner this entire human world is getting merged with that shape.

Uddhav remained gazing.

Now, only the two eyes of Akroor could be seen above the water. There was a quiver among the rings. Akroor raised his right hand from amidst the flow; a sound manifested..."May there be well-being."

"Just as the wind blowing in the forests does not get delighted and remaining with fire, it does not get depressed…just as despite the sky being all pervasive is unattached and boundless…just as the earth bears all the creatures...yet…only man is dependent on his deeds! water is purifying and also dynamic in the same way, a renounced person should accept the truth principle of the continuity of Soul…Fire…even after swallowing the entire creation still remains hungry…."

It was as if the sound of Yamuna's flow had changed. The bells tied to the cows' necks standing on the banks tingled. Uddhav folded his hands bent his head; the rings around the flow had now changed—a void-like state rose up for a moment and then the flow returned to its earlier way. Akroor had self immolation in that flow.

"Krishna…Krishna!" Uddhav closed his eyes, "What you had said, these are those five elements!" and…and… becoming depressed, offered a handful of water in his cupped palms as sacrificial oblations.

"O Revered Akroor! May you rest in the universal god. Somaaya…Agnaye…yamaaya…svadhaa namaha..." (सोमाय …अग्नये…यमाय…स्वधा नमः ।)

The sun was rising on the eastern horizon. Uddhav looked at the direction of Mathura. Last night when he had entered Mathura…that hour came back to his memory. Now there was no one remaining who would recognize him.

Uddhav cast his sight in the direction of Gokul; he began looking longingly at the dust on the path. Krishna had come to Mathura by this path only and now, on the same path in the same dust, Uddhav's steps will move forward.

The pasturage of the cows could be seen from far off. Uddhav's steps slowed down a bit. The path towards the Vrajabhoomi also digressed from here only. Uddhav was standing at the three fold path—Mathura as left behind…to the right and left Gokul and the Vraja were shining, akin to the two shining eyes of Uddhav.

The Yamuna was in front in whose flow Akroor had merged just a little while back.

Uddhav was sitting on a rock on its banks.

There was a little stirring between the small trees and the tall grass. Uddhav looked at it—a snake quickly slid away in another direction. Uddhav's eyes beamed. He suddenly recollected the Kaaliya Naag. Here only standing somewhere nearby, once Krishna had asked Uddhav—

"Uddhav! In this burning heat of the sun instead of filling water from this water source of Yamuna so near; why are the milk-maids going so far away?"

Uddhav had replied, "The Kaaliya Naag has blocked the flow of Yamuna near the Vrajabhoomi. It is his rule over this water source. O Damodar, he is very dangerous. He does not allow the milk-maids of Gokul to take even a drop of water from his water source."

"How is the rule of anyone possible over the Yamuna, Uddhav?" Krishna asked in wonder, "When there is a reservoir of water so near to the village houses and the milk-maids have to take so much trouble in the burning heat of the sun? this...this…is gross injustice."

"I do not know much about justice and injustice Krishna..." Uddhav said maintaining his decorum, "I only know this much that this Gokul's reservoir of water is out of bounds to the residents of Gokul because there is the powerful rule of Kaliya Naag over it."

"Air, water, earth, sky and the sun—these are the five great basic elements, Uddhav!"

Krishna was making some decisive observation, "How can there be anybody's rule over them? Protecting them is essential for the benefit of everyone for everyone's happiness—and that should apply to the entire macrocosm! This water reservoir must be freed. All of us together shall defeat Kaaliya."

Seeing the brightness which arose in Krishna's eyes, Uddhav's eyes became bewildered.

And that very moment, Kaaliya really got defeated... That moment....

As if nothing special had indeed occurred and smiling with such ease, Krishna looked at the residents of Vraja standing on the banks; the defeated and ashamed Kaaliya was standing there itself. Krishna was still holding his hood with one hand.

"Kaaliya!" said Krishna, in such a way that everyone could hear him, "Defeat is not of your power, it is of your attitude. Once you become free of your impure actions then that change will transform defeat into victory. Go...never again pollute this water flow; I am leaving you free."

Released from the grip of Krishna—Kaaliya looked at the human community for a moment, glanced once at Krishna and then moved forward in the direction of the North.

"Krishna!" Balaram was revealing the anxiety present in everybody's minds, "Kaaliya will now become safe among his own kith and kin in the Khandav forest; what if this safe enemy converts the entire Khandav forest into our enemies?"

Krishna laughed out...that same carefree laughter! "Brother! We have not seen the Khandav forest and if Kaaliya retains the memory of the old enmity; then the fate of the Khandav forest will also become the same which has now become of Kaaliya's rule."

Uddhav turned his face all around in a detached manner. Many years back Krishna had sent him to Gokul that incident...now came up in front of his eyes—Once Krishna left Gokul and went to Mathura...he sank so much in Mathura's diplomacy that he never got free time to even look in this direction. At that time Uddhav had become Krishna's messenger and come here...and today, after so many years he will step into Gokul....

Uddhav became a bit uneasy. Just the previous night when he had entered Mathura, he was a stranger to everyone…now…now…how many generations of Gokul's cowherd men and women would have passed…just one Radha, yes…just one Radha—surely Radha will recognize him! If perhaps Radha also….

Uddhav became ashamed at his own thoughts. On that unforgettable night of the Raas-leela, Radha had told Uddhav—"Uddhav! That moment when the atmosphere of Gokul's community becomes free from that moment… Radha's name will also be attached with that atmosphere… don't forget this!"

Uddhav felt uneasy; he was able to recover his composure with difficulty from his eagerness to roll in that very same dust…. Where there was no one, there only he could see everything as his own.

His contemplation lost itself in the abyss of the past.

□

19

Destroying the Republic Kansa usurped to throne of Mathura and then…the community of Gokul began hurting him as if it was a loss of prestige. Till now the relation between Gokul and Mathura was that of a strong elder and younger brother. The community of Gokul was free and happy under the leadership of Nandbaba. But Kansa tightened his clutches over it. The powerful Magadh kingdom was under him. Jarasandh's daughters were queens in the harem of Kansa hence his father-in-law's full support was available to him. And that is another reason why Gokul's independence was hurting him all the more. Kansa sent message to Nandbaba, "accept my rule and regularly send ghee, milk, butter to Mathura."

Nandbaba got afraid. To confront that power who had dissolved the Yadava assembly of Mathura was difficult for the community of Gokul. After mutual consultations, it was decided that the community of Gokul would accept the rule of Mathura and send dairy products regularly to Kansa in a symbolic form…and that routine also commenced.

When teenaged Krishna saw for the first time the milk-producing vessels going towards Mathura, he was astonished. Why is this invaluable prosperity going in the direction of Mathura? Instead of this sweet milk of his dear cows going to the cowherd boys and to the cowherd women and men of Gokul, why is it going for the citizens of Mathura? Those cows whose well-being, whose protection and the care takers of their love were the residents of Gokul...why? Why this symbol of love of those cows are transferred elsewhere? What kind of justice is this?

"Brother!" Krishna asked this question to Balaram, "That milk which the cowherd-maids of Gokul prepared, its use instead of us, why should it be used by the residents of Mathura? Without spoiling even a drop of their effort's-sweat? This is a great injustice!"

Instead of Balaram, Nandbaba explained to Krishna, "The kingdom of Mathura is very powerful, and this powerful kingdom, always has an upper hand. Where is the power in Gokul to disregard Kansa?"

The young Krishna could not digest this matter. He again placed his question in front of Balaram, Uddhav, and the other cowherds and teen agers friends.

"The Gokul community is ours and the cows' milk is indeed its prosperity. If a powerful man keeps snatching it away then won't we be considered to be cowards? The milk products of our cows should be availed by us. We shall stop it..." said Krishna explaining to everyone.

"Krishna..." said a senior friend pointing out the flaw in the plan, "Even if we all become united without the co-operation of the milk-maids this task is impossible. A firm fear has taken roots in the minds of the women...that if we make even a little lapse in delivering the milk products in Kansa's mansion then, the fate of Nandbaba along with all the cowherd-men will be the same as what happened to the Yadavas of Mathura. Ugrasen, Vasudeva and others who are rotting in the prison."

"Then we shall make all the milk-maids fearless. Let us explain to them also the viewpoint of Dharma and justice..." said Krishna.

"It is difficult to collect the women together and to explain to them the importance of this message in these manner. For achieving this task if we have some energetic maidens on our side then perhaps the task can be done.

Through this maidens we can gather all the women and put before them the point of view of Dharma and justice."

"Such an energetic maidens?"

"Vrajapur's prominent personage, Vrishabhaanu and Kritika's daughter, Radha…."

"Radha?" Krishna's smile bloomed, "She is the wife of the senior cowherd Raayan…."

The day on which he had defeated the Kaaliya Naag at that time…seeing the struggling shape in his clutches and standing amidst the wonder struck, frightened and fascinated group of Gokul residents…was Radha...her remembrance came back to Krishna! There was mixed feelings in everyone's eyes but only the eyes of the one and only Radha was glimmering with confidence towards this spectacle of Krishna. Those eyes filled with confidence were looking at Krishna in a fixed gaze. Those eyes came back to Krishna's memory. Such feeling inspired eyes; Krishna had never seen such eyes which went deep into one's soul. If Radha will support him in this task then….

—In that case not only for the people of Gokul, but even for the re-establishment of the freedom of Mathura's Republic the task would become easy. Radha should gather together the women of Gokul and if Krishna can give these women the message of fearlessness and justice… then probably the entire task can be accomplished. By the sacrifice of the residents of Gokul and their Dharma inspired struggle, even if only immediate gains could be achieved… but...the re-etablishment of long-lasting fearlessness of society can be achieved…only through women. In order to make this thought reach up to the women, there was none better than Radha. The confidence with which she had fixed her gaze on Krishna that same confidence can help in this struggle.

This suggestion of Radha's co-operation seemed good to Krishna. Krishna would never delay any of his plans. He met Radha and explained the whole matter to her.

"Radha!" Krishna said in the end, "Without your co-operation this herculean task cannot be accomplished."

"Can any task be herculean for the Krishna who had defeated the powerful enemy like Kaaliya?", saying so Radha laughed. In her laughter and in her eyes, Krishna could see confidence and an ocean of emotion sparkiling.

"Yes Radha! Single handedly it is not easy to defeat the enemy. The task of welfare of the macrocosm cannot be handled alone by Krishna—For that…Krishna needs Radha also".

"Krishna's flute and Krishna's peacock feather are indeed all pervasive Keshav! If Radha can become merely an instrument, it would be her great fortune."

There was nothing further to be said which needed words and voice; Krishna himself completed the subject.

"Gathering the females folks on the next full-moon night in the banks of Kalindi and the task of conveying Krishna's message to them…."

"Radha will do it..." Radha stood bowing her head in front of Krishna.

Not half but the entire Gokul had come and was standing on the banks of Kalindi. That Krishna's flute sings out such sweet music for the first time…all of them got the experience of it that day. The female folks were swaying. The white brightness which was flowing from the sky was as if it was creating two parallel rivers. Radha had indeed spoken the truth that Krishna's flute and Krishna's peacock feather were indeed all pervasive and Krishna's statement also was as much truth that without Radha, his tune and colour does not make any sense at all…. Each and every young woman was swaying with Krishna's tune and this tune message had become echo like.

Uddhav had sunk into the memory of that wonderful Raas-leela, and an understanding arose—O My God! What a great far-seer Krishna was! (आर्षद्रष्टा). Had not the tune of Dharma and fearlessness reached the hearts of the women of the community through his flute then? How would have Yashoda agreed to send Krishna with Akroor to Mathura? And if Krishna had not gone to Mathura then?

Uddhav closed his eyes—Then probably the Kalindi would not have been flowing.... Probably that Vraja located Govardhan would not have been standing up this way... with his head standing up so high....

The huge Yamalaarjun trees would have remained standing blocking the road today also, and...the milk trapped in the injustice form vessels would have continued to go round and round on the road from Gokul to Mathura....

But had Krishna not got the support of Radha then how would this have been possible? Would Krishna has been able to do all this without Radha?—this question arose in Uddhav's mind and simultaneously he got the answer to another question which had been rising in Uddhav's mind since many days. Those last moments while abandoning the five elemental body and at that time Radha being remembered by Krishna.... Why? Why? All of a sudden the answer to Uddhav's question was found. Even the name Radha was transporting Uddhav somewhere.... The Krishna who went to participate in Kansa's Yajna from Gokul to Mathura after that, never again did he meet Radha never again did he place his foot on the earth of Gokul and...and...today? The news of that Krishna renouncing his body is to be given to Radha, who continually for so many years, is sitting dissolved in Krishna...in whose life that page opened...which never again closed...on which was written, KRISHNA!

Uddhav's mind was filled with sadness.

Krishna went to Mathura; after the killing of Kansa with the invasion of Jarasandh, Krishna got engaged in the defence of Mathura. Then he went to Dwaraka, Indraprasth, Praagjyotishpur—a continual travel, search as if he had pervaded everywhere. But Radha never went out of the limits of Gokul. In the atmosphere of Gokul, in the leaves of the trees here, in the bellows of the cows, in the gurgling sound of Yamuna; she constantly saw Krishna only.... Probably, Radha is even now waiting for him! hoping that sometime or other some chariot would bring Krishna back to Gokul.

Departing from Gokul...with the remembrance of this, the hour to leave Mathura made its appearance; Krishna's Gokul renounciation was a very significant step for the benefit of the collectivity. But Krishna's Mathura renunciation was a chapter of the selfishness and meanness of that very collectivity. That Mathura, to which Krishna gave back its freedom had re-established the prominent Yadava personages once again on important positions of the Republic, that very Mathura, the very same prominent Yadavas told Krishna—"Krishna! Now you are not needed. You go away from here."

At that time also Uddhav was present in the Yadava assembly. That Krishna who had made the Raas-leela an instrument to spread the message of justice and fearlessness in the women of the community; Uddhav had seen That Krishna. Defeating Kansa within the wink of an eye and the Krishna who had once again revived the Republic of Mathura...Uddhav had seen? also...and...and...now expelled by the same Republic and those very Mathura residents. Uddhav had seen That Krishna also leaving Mathura and going away.

Why did Krishna who constantly fought for the sake of Dharma and justice, himself have to face such indifference? Without seeking anything for himself...he chose the path of justice; in that why did he have to drink the poison of injustice?

A commotion rose in Uddhav's mind.

As soon as the news of Kansa's killing crossed the borders and reached the ears of the king of Magadh Jarasandh, fire flared up in his body mind. He had given his two daughters to Kansa in marriage and through this Kansa, Jarasandh wanted to uproot all-prevailing republics in the entire Aaryavart. Suddenly, Krishna had shattered this dream. And then this also came into his mind that the Krishna, who brought back republicanism in Mathura... will tomorrow show this path to the subjects of Magadh and Aaryavart also. Today Kansa was killed, tomorrow Shishupal, Paundrak or Jarasandh will be killed. Jarasandh recognized the birth of a fearsome enemy in the form of Krishna; the killer of Kansa, this Krishna should be finished off! Jarasandh gathered his army and with full power attacked Mathura.

The Yadava assembly of Mathura had indeed foreseen the attack by Jarasandh. How can Jarasandh bear the widowhood of his daughters. The power of Mathura which was lying in a state of unconsciousness till today by the killing of Kansa became alive again. Mathura was becoming as if it was in a state of eagerness to fight with Jarasandh with the support of Krishna.

Such a massive counter attack was beyond Jarasandh's imagination. His dream to destroy Mathura within a moment became scattered. The Yadavas who were fighting under the leadership of Krishna were totally different from the Yadavas who fought under the leadership of Ugrasen; Jarasandh understood this and he immediately made a new formation of his forces for attack.

The king of Sindhudesh, Kaalayavan was an enemy of the Yadavas. The purohit of the Yadavas had insulted Kaalayavan's father Maharshi Gaargya. On account of this insult, the offended Gaargya had given order to Kaalayavan—"Son! Your indebtedness towards your father will be completed when you crush the Yadavas". Jarasandh contacted Kaalayavan. The attack by Sindhudesh from the North of Mathura and from the South and East the Magadh army's attack. That's it...Mathura will be fully surrounded; the helpless Krishna will be destroyed—

thus an understanding was arrived at between Jarasandh and Kaalayavan.

After crossing over the Syamant Panchak region, Kaalayavan of Sindhudesh was coming running in the large open areas of Aaryavart; when this news reached Mathura the Yadava assembly became restless. Only Krishna alone was composed.

Did Krishna not have any fear even while colliding with powerful and brave persons like Shishupal, Paundrak, or Bhasmaasur? Justice and Dharma was on the side of Mathura. As far as numbers are concerned, this side may very well seem to be less but its defeat is not possible... Krishna's full confidence was over it. In fact, from the Kaaliya serpent till Kansa, everyone was powerful even then all of them were defeated; because Dharma and justice were on the side of Krishna.

However, Kaalavayan's attack on Aaryavart was a new development. Dharma and justice were still on the side of Mathura...but...this arrival of Kaalayavan amounted to interference by a foreigner from across the Sindhudesh in an internal conflict. And once this foreign interference enters into this internal conflict then? What to talk of Mathura's republic, it would be difficult for even the Magadha kingdom to survive. Due to selfishness and anger, there was only the attitude of revenge in the eyes of Jarasandh; it was the great future approaching in front of Krishna and that was next day's morning.

A big danger arose once again. Three directions into Mathura is getting closed. Ugrasen and Vasudeva's intellect was not working. In the assembly which had been called to discuss the matter, one senior Yadava by name Vikadru, said in a loud voice, "Krishna! By this attack by Jarasandh the survival of Mathura seems to be difficult."

"I know my limits, O Revered Sir!" Krishna said with a composed mind but with seriousness, "I wish to seek your blessings and guidance."

"Kaalayavan is unconquerable and Jarasandh has become blind with rage" said Vikadru assessing the situation, "You freed Mathura from the authority of Kansa and revived the dead republic; not only Mathura the entire Aaryavart will remain indebted to you for this uncomparable contribution of your...Krishna…but...but...."

"What? what but? O Revered Sir.... Why did you stop? Please tell unhesitatingly." Krishna reassured him.

"Krishna!" said Vikadru hesitantly.

"Jarasandh's enmity is not with Mathura…it is with Krishna..." saying so Krishna completed the sentence.

"Krishna you released Mathura once—by killing Kansa." Said Vikadru taking his opinion forward, "Only you can release it a second time also Krishna." Vikadru's speech got stuck.

"How O Revered Sir? It will not be a burden on Krishna to make any sacrifice for the sake of Mathura..you…please say it."

"Leaving Mathura if you go away in some unknown direction then Jarasandh and Kaalayavan would drop the attack on Mathura and go after you; Krishna, they desire you, they have enmity towards you." saying so Vikadru completed his talk.

Complete silence spread over the Yadava assembly.

Tears wailed up in Uddhav's eyes. The entire atmosphere became still; it appeared as if the sky had forgotten to wink its eyes.

That Mathura which Krishna had revived that very same Mathura is today asking Krishna to leave Mathura….

"What you are saying is true, O Revered Sir." Standing with folded hands and bent head in front of the Yadava assembly, Krishna said, "I myself had told Kansa that the republic is greater than the individual! I had never thought that I will have to confirm my words through my actions so soon. This is indeed my fortune…I, my elder brother and some Yadava friends shall leave Mathura early in the morning; we are surrounded from three sides but the western direction is open. I shall leave by that direction in such a way that Kaalayavan and Jarasandh would see me running away...."

Completing his talk Krishna looked at all Yadavas. Everyone's face was smeared black; everyone's eyes had turned down.

Next day early morning Krishna left the town from the western gate. Seeing Krishna running away, Jarasandh's army let out a victory cry. Kaalayavan ran after Krishna. Krishna's smile became vocal and his movement became fast; Mathura was saved from total destruction.

Each and every hair pore of the western Aaryavart bloomed with an unknown delight; bright light spread in the direction of Dwaraka.

By the remembrance of that difficult hour of the past, Uddhav became distressed. For a long time, he was sitting on that rock with a void head. That's it...within a short while he will meet Radha; only that one task was left to convey the message of Krishna's body dissolution to Radha; after conveying that he himself also will become detached from the entire past. Now no other thread remains to join with the past.

Getting up slowly Uddhav dipped his feet in Kalindi's flow. By the coolness of water, he got peace. Standing in the middle of the flow he had a sip of water; saluted the sun and then moved forward in the direction of Gokul.

"Whose house are you searching Maharaj?"

Uddhav got startled. So he had already entered Gokul. The time for twilight to spring out had come. The lanes were resounding with the jingling sound of the bells of the cows returning home and their bellowing and the screaming of the calves. Moving each step forward with speed, Uddhav's eyes...though seeing them all were not seeing anything; That's all...he was searching for Radha's house.

"Whose house are you searching Maharaj?" the question was repeated. This time the cowherd boy asking the question was standing in front of him. Uddhav turned his sight on his face. The face appeared totally strange. There was no sign of recognition even on the faces of the other cowherd boys standing nearby. Uddhav was a stranger in Gokul. Now, here he was merely "Maharaj"!

Uddhav's lips twitched—"I am not a stranger in Gokul, Brother! don't worry, I am searching for my own house; I shall find it."

The cowherd boys did not say anything further. Looking at one another they went their way. Slowly, Uddhav came near Raayaan's house and stood there.

It was already evening at that time; a conch sounded from somewhere near the banks of Kalindi. Sound from the clock arose; there was a quiver in the atmosphere. Uddhav was looking at the raised verandah. A vast tree's shadow had spread itself on the verandah in such a way, appearing as if some mother was fondling her child on her lap. From somewhere the sound of the flow of milk falling into vessels from the cows' udder, could be heard; this sound, this tree. Oh my God! This open space of Raayan's house, the sound of the conch—nothing had changed in Gokul.... The bellowing of the cows, the mischief of the calves pulling milk from the udders of their mothers—everything was the same and yet today, Uddhav was a traveller. A stranger.

"Whom do you want to meet Maharaj?" asked an elderly women who was coming out of Raayan's house looking at Uddhav.

Uddhav again got startled. Now that woman coming out from the dim light was standing right in front of Uddhav.

"Raayan and Radha." Uddhav muttered.

"Raayaan!" that woman's eyes blinked with surprise—"You? from where are you coming Maharaj? Lot of time has passed since Raayaan left for heaven."

Uddhav closed his eyes—from somewhere within he shivered. It was as if Raayaan's five elemental body appeared alive in front of him—now this Raayaan is also not there, Nandbaba is also not there, mother Yashoda has also bid farewell; Krishna also had dropped his body,

Sankarshan Balaram has also gone…and that tree…both remained looking at one another.

"There…there is no need to tell Radha" that elderly woman laughed out, "See…there you see Radha; she has become old, husband has gone, even then she does not leave decorating herself with flowers and neither does she leave smearing sandal paste. See…how she is standing adorned with ornaments, just see…."

Uddhav saw.

Yes, it was indeed Radha. She is not an old widow which this old woman telling about…. She is just as she was at the time of Raas-leela on the bank of Kalindi; Yes, she has become a bit weak! Her attire, ornaments, sandal-past smear, glower garland—everything was as fresh as it was then. The smile on her face has not disappeared. The very same faith in her eyes, the same adoration was gleaming…. There was no expectation; there was no worry. She was the personification of simplicity and utter peace.

Uddhav remained stunned. The years that had gone by in the mean time. A complete epoch did not pass away! The destiny come to a standstill! Gokul, Mathura, Dwaraka, Hastinapur—everything had changed!—beginning with grandsire or beginning with father Vasudeva up to Uddhav himself and there again…till that Ashwatthama… sequentially destiny had taken away everyone in a small or larger manner…and this span of time did not so much as even touch Radha? This Radha has become untouchable even by this flow of time….

"Radha!" indistinct tone came out of Uddhav.

"Who? Uddhav?" a counter question could be heard from Radha. Uddhav was standing in a little darkness. Radha did not have even an inkling of his coming. By just the one word that had come out from his lips, how did Radha recognize him? Uddhav became overwhelmed.

It was as if Arjuna's despondency on the first day of the beginning of Kurukshetra war was recurring; it was in that manner in which Uddhav kept looking at Radha with unblinking eyes. It was indeed Krishna himself who had sent Uddhav to Gokul many years back. Conveying the message of Krishna, he had consoled Nandji, Yashoda, Radha and all others. It was as if the lamp flame of the spiritless Gokul was lit again by the message of Uddhav; such was the manner in which it had begun sparkling again.

Uddhav observed that the elderly woman had no interest in Radha's talks. She went away from there.

"Radha..." asked Uddhav carefully observing Radha who was standing near, "Hope all is well with you?"

Radha laughed out—the same innocent laugh. Even her laughter had not changed a bit.... The fragrance of sandalwood and flowers was coming from her body.

"You are asking about Radha's well-being, Uddhav? It was only yesterday that you had come from Mathura with Krishna's message, then...."

"Only yesterday?" Uddhav was startled. "What are you telling Radha? Have you forgotten the time ocean of a complete epoch's time span?"

"Why forget?" Radha laughed again. This time her laughter had spread wide on her mouth; it was if she was mocking at Uddhav, "It appears as if old age has crept over you Uddhav; tell me what message have you brought me about Krishna?"

"Yes Radha..." Uddhav said slowly, "this time it is indeed my task to convey Krishna's message to you.... Krishna's message."

"Tell me Uddhav, tell me quickly..." for the first time Radha became a bit restless, "Please do not delay in conveying Krishna's message!"

"Radha!" with much feeling Uddhav placed his hand on Radha's head, "Krishna...Krishna has said...." But words again got stuck up.

"What has Krishna said Uddhav, what has Krishna said?" Radha was staring at Uddhav with unblinking eyes.

"Krishna has said that...that...'Radha...! Krishna is not there now...'" even in climbing the Himalaya's steep incline it had not taken so much effort, as much as it took for Uddhav to complete one sentence. Uddhav was completely exhausted.

"Krishna is not there?" Radha burst out laughing, "What is this you are saying Uddhav? Krishna himself told that…'Krishna is not there?' and to say this little news why did he send you? Waah...! How curious! 'Krishna is not there'!" Radha went on laughing freely.

"Radha…you…you…don't understand anything!" Uddhav fell into a dilemma. The news which he has to tell Radha, with that he was so much distressed…and...and... here? there is no value for that news! "Why…why…are you laughing so much?"

"You are telling news which is worth laughing at, Uddhav!" curbing her laughter with difficulty Radha said, "Have you seen this sky Uddhav?" suddenly raising her eyes up, showed him the sky.

"Sky?" Uddhav turned his eyes towards the sky… one or two stars had come out. Like the flowers braided on Radha's head, these stars in the sky….

"And there can you see the Kalindi?" Radha asked the next question.

In that deepening darkness Uddhav saw the Kalindi shining like silver lining.

"And this wind—and there…near the tree...those peacock feathers—you are able to see all these isn't it?" Radha asked Uddhav bringing her mouth close to Uddhav's ear.

"Radha, what is all this you are saying?"

"You are seeing all these with your eyes and still you are saying that Krishna is not there…! Is this not a laughing matter Uddhav? Surely, old age has disillusioned you!" said Radha.

"Radha…Radha! why don't you understand?" Uddhav became restless, "Krishna's five elemental body is not there amidst us now..." finally Uddhav said that...that…which he was hesitating to tell….

Radha suddenly became solemn; without blinking she began staring at Uddhav.

"Krishna's five elemental body?" Radha caught hold of Uddhav's hand, "Come, Uddhav come, just now Krishna was here only; come, let me take you to him..." so saying Radha got hold of Uddhav and pulled him. Uddhav's legs staggered a bit, he got pulled by the fast moving steps of Radha.

"Radha…Radha…what is this you are saying?" tried stopping her during most of the way.

But Radha moved on as if she heard nothing. She continued to walk fast. Uddhav had no other alternative than to follow Radha. The echo from their feet went on rising in the calm lanes of Gokul…went on rising….

"Oh! This is the same ascetic!" said some one from the crowd in front seeing Uddhav. Uddhav looked in the direction from which the voice came—but could not see the face.

"And where is this stranger sage going with this mad woman at this time?" someone asked the question.

Mad Radha?!

Uddhav's legs stopped.

He was nothing more than a stranger ascetic in Gokul!

Radha went on as if she did had not heard anything, had not see anyone; she kept walking with steady steps. Uddhav stopped a little behind.

"O Brother!" going near the cowherd Uddhav asked, "Why are you calling Radha mad?"

"If not mad then what Maharaj?" someone said, "Her husband has died yet she does not leave her adornment…. Now you yourself tell, if a widow wears such attire, does such adornment then…what is she? if not mad?"

Radha was a widow!

□

20

Uddhav sank into reflection for a moment. In front of eyes appeared widow women without the symbol of a married woman. How can Radha also be a widow like them? Other signs related with widowhood...like disappointment, old age looks, signs of helplessness! none of these signs were there in Radha. Oh! so much so...that Radha remained untouched even by time. She was as she was years back—composed, young, full of consciousness and drowned in surrender.

How did this become possible?

Does time span also ever stops?

"Uddhav!" piercing through the darkness Radha's voice was heard. Uddhav moved his steps forward.

On the banks of Kalindi coming under the open skies Radha stood there.

"Here is Krishna, Uddhav, here he is!" facing Uddhav Radha said, "You are seeing this sky isn't it? You are seeing the flowing Kalindi isn't it? You are seeing those leaves of that tamaal tree fluttering isn't it?—All these are there and you are saying that Krishna is not there? How is this possible Uddhav? What? What? Are you able to see only the five elemental body of Krishna?

"We are all donning body Radha..." said Uddhav.

"Even after the contact with Krishna...this consciousness still remains fixed on a separate body...this is a matter of great surprise Uddhav!" Radha again burst out laughing.

It was as if Uddhav became completely wet in the flow of that laughter. Purer than the flow of Kalindi…this flow of Radha's laughter was far more placid.

Uddhav felt—Radha's greatness was even higher than the height of the sky.

"See there Uddhav!" Radha suddenly drew Uddhav's attention. Uddhav saw, under a Pippal tree, a big stone which had become soggy due to the flow of Kalindi was lying there.

"The day all of you went with Akroorji in Kansa's Yajna to Mathura, from the night of the next day, under the shadow of this tree's leaves…in the presence of this stone… everything is florid Uddhav! Krishna was sitting here itself like this, just see here." Radha catching Uddhav's hand again took him and went. Uddhav remained seeing with wide open eyes; kept walking.

Arjuna was saying—that he had offered Krishna's body to the five elements in the Prabhas kshetra. Arjuna himself had told this to Uddhav. The body which had dissolved in the five elements—can it again become visible like this? Radha is telling the truth. Did Krishna really sit on this stone? Uddhav rubbed his eyes.

Krishna who was ready to go in Kansa's yajna with Akroor had bid farewell to everybody. Moistening everyone from the Kadamba tree to the cows…with the exception of one…Radha. The whole day Krishna could not see Radha anywhere.

Krishna was to bid farewell next day early morning. As the night advanced, Gokul became calm and the waters of Yamuna also flowed sluggishly as if tired…at that time Krishna had come here to bid farewell to Radha under this Pippal tree in front of the flow of Kalindi. Hiding herself from everyone since the whole day, with tear filled eyes Radha was waiting here itself for Krishna since evening. She was not prepared for this farewell in any way; the moment

Krishna tells her, "Radha, I am going!" that moment will not merely be a fraction of time, but…it will be an explosion, shattering the universe she herself will be shred to pieces.

But that fearsome moment which she was trying to avoid did at last arrive…. At mid-night to bid farewell to Radha, searching for her Krishna reached here.

"Radha!" said Krishna with the same calmness and with a delightful tenderness, "early in the morning I shall leave for Mathura; the entire Gokul has bid me farewell, now even you…Radha...you…."

"Farewell?" Radha stared at Krishna with unblinking eyes.

"Yes, Radha! One has to after all remain under the compulsion of the deeds of this birth, isn't it?"

"I have nothing to say regarding the cycle of deeds Krishna!" said Radha, "But for that, is it unavoidable that Radha bids farewell to Krishna? Radha can never bid you farewell. Don't you know this Janardan?"

"I know, Radha! and know this also that my going to Mathura is not any ordinary event…."

"Meaning?"

"Every relation is bound by deeds Radha! Living inert, having body-bodiless, gross-subtle—all these are bound by deeds. The end of all these is certain. Gross and subtle, everything comes to an end." Krishna went on speaking, "To accept this end gracefully—this is humanism."

"Even after accepting the humanism, the observance one loftier-dharma remains Krishna! It is that very dharma, which is stopping Radha from bidding farewell to Krishna…."

"Radha!" said Krishna, "After my departure to Mathura my returning to Gokul is not destined in the book of future…. After bidding farewell from here all these relations and this entire creation—all these will get detached from Krishna's life."

"Krishna...!" for the first time Radha got disturbed, "That 'you yourself and even Krishna should be detached from Gokul'…such a future...?"

"Yes Radha, such is fated…. Who can indeed win over the ultimate? Even the relation of Radha and Krishna today, now…this very moment will arrive at a full stop Radha...! Now Krishna will never be able to meet Radha. This is indeed the indication of the beginning of the new era Radha…bid me farewell…" said Krishna.

"That destiny which even Krishna cannot cross over to comprehend that deed is impossible for Radha…" she said, "But…but...at this gross moment of completion an intense desire has arisen Krishna; I cannot be freed of a human desire."

"What such desire is there Radha? What such desire is troubling you?"

"Krishna!" said Radha becoming extremely emotional. Her voice became unsteady.

"How is it possible for me to stop you? Yes, who indeed has been able to stop the future…. But in the hour of this last meeting I have one desire Krishna! Let me…let me... placing my head at your feet, let me shed some tears; that's all! then this Radha will become bodiless; no one will be able to detach her from Krishna...."

A smile bloomed over Krishna's face. Radha kept looking at him with unblinking eyes.

The mid sky moon was reflecting in the Kalindi. The cool breeze of the early morning had begun descending in the air.

Without speaking a word Krishna sat upon the stone. Radha bent at Krishna's feet…that was the first touch… the embodied Krishna and Radha…Radha's touch on the feet and the sprinkling of the tears…the first expression of human love. A smile kept playing on Krishna's lips; the peacock feather kept fluttering in the air. After many years destiny was to appear on the horizon. The moment of that early morning on the bank of the confluence of Hiral and Kapila rivers was shaped unknowingly. It had just arrived on the banks of Kalindi, making Jaraa the hunter an instrument, the location where the arrow of destiny will pierce on Krishna's body…that location was also finalized at that very moment….

"Uddhav!" said Radha, "That hour in which Krishna went to Mathura, that very hour Krishna pervaded Radha's being in her each and every hair pore…the Krishna of Gokul, was visible now this Krishna, every moment was present everywhere. At the time of bidding farewell Krishna had said…."

"What had he said Radha?" asked Uddhav.

"Krishna had said, 'Radha...! As long as you keep this fragrance permeating you, no one will be able to separate you from Krishna…. Even destiny remembering this moment…will stand still O Radha...!" Radha continued, "these ornaments, these flower garlands, this sandal paste smear and this beautiful dress; all these were very dear to Krishna, Uddhav!—Very dear…. That moment I was in this attire form…and that is why that same Radha is continuing to re-live that very moment in the presence of that very Krishna; see Uddhav…Krishna renounced only them who had bid him farewell…" Saying this much Radha again burst out laughing so loud that Uddhav was taken aback and…the ocean wailed up in Radha's eyes unrestricted….

Uddhav got the answer to a moment, question also which was playing in his mind since many days—Why Krishna remembered Radha in his last hour?

Now no question remained unanswered nor any confusion or complication.

"O Uddhav! What are we searching for in this creation, which emanated from void and whose end is also in void? Between the beginning and end of void what else but void can be there?"—The fast flowing waters of Alaknanda, the echo-producing Himalaya mountains and the huge rocks—even in that resounding abyss, it was as if Uddhav was hearing only Krishna's voice. On the eve of taking the Yadavas to the Prabhas-kshetra calling Uddhav, Krishna had indicated to Uddhav to proceed on pilgrimage. Uddhav recollected that hour. Krishna will now never return on Dwaraka's land—Uddhav's mind had surmised at that time itself; the echo of that dialogue was as if it was manifesting from the Alaknanda and knocking against the snow clad peaks of the Himalayas—Uddhav was listening to that.

After conveying the message of Krishna's dropping the body to Radha, Uddhav had taken the path to the Himalayas. Now there was no location left on the earth, no name left…Oh...! what to talk of location and name where is the world also now left in the universe? Everything was formless nameless…Radha was completely dissolved in Krishna—a complete union…. For her the message of Krishna bidding farewell was like a meaningless dialogue.... Uddhav was left astonished…now there was no scale for time, there was only an echo like fate…Uddhav turned his back to these memories.

Having bath and contemplating in the rivers of Yamuna, Ganges, Mandakini—which were flowing, pulling the coolness of the Himalayas with them...Uddhav had now reached the Badridham, near the origin of Alaknanda. In front of the holy Badri temple of Badridham, standing near the hot-springs, Uddhav ran his gaze upon the vast borders of Nature. The Vasudhaara stream was not very far off, descending from the mountains in front, were the Rigved-current and the Yajurved-current and the green forest region spread over for miles together…and touching all these, there was the stream of pure solitude….

"…making the body a medium, perform your duty Uddhav! No allurement towards the body nor its renunciation…. If you ponder in solitude then this truth will reveal itself faster….

That solitude which Krishna had considered as witness of ultimate, is this 'that solitude'? Whatever Krishna had told Uddhav; why is the experience of 'that' taking place so fast at this moment? Uddhav was overwhelmed...! The vibrations of Krishna's utterance was ringing here as if blending form colour fragrance".

Uddhav's eyes became fixed on the mountains.

He got the impression of some sound emanating from the snow clad mountain peaks. Over the melting snow, prints of someone's feet was seen.... Could these footprints be Krishna's? or else?

Uddhav recollected Vasudeva—recollection of mother Devaki. Rukimini and Satyabhama, Arjuna, Ashwatthama—Akroor and—and...Radha—whose feet could have been imprinted over the divine peaks of the Himalayas?

He looked at his face in the hot-spring. It was after seeing his face in this water only that Narada had been freed from delusion—that is why this spring is termed as Narad kund. Narada's face was now not to be seen anywhere in the Narad kund but Uddhav felt—how can delusion remain here? even for a moment?

From the hour Arjuna had told Uddhav the news of Krishna's dropping his body, from that moment itself a deep void had surrounded Uddhav. In the banks of the Ganges, Arjuna had told about the beginning of a Krishna devoid epoch; even a erudite like Uddhav had never imagined about a Krishna devoid epoch. That which was beyond imagination, that was indeed the truth. A great era had already set and it was as if Uddhav was absorbing this setting mountain since many days. The entire Nature was That itself—the sun, moon, stars, air, sky, flowing rivers and these forests and jungles—everything—as they were...and yet there was everywhere an invasion of void. Even the colours of the peacock or else the sound of the flute coming up from somewhere—even all these did not seem as they used to earlier. Even the shivering of a cow's body skin and the bellowing of the calves were as if they had changed. In front of Uddhav's eyes, the bewilderment of Arjuna, the shriek of Ashwatthama, Akroor'a pain... and...and....

The still Tamaal tree of the Vrajabhoomi, the leaves of the Kadamba, the rocks and stones of the Govardhan—all... all were rising up as if trembling.

"Uddhav! There is no Dharma more valuable than love and compassion. This is indeed justice, this is Dharma.... Infatuation is attachment...and attachment less love is indeed compassion." Krishna had said and he was after all a far seeing sage.... He had known Uddhav's future right from the beginning. Even before void and attachment could surround Uddhav...he had cautioned Uddhav....

And yet till he had met Radha, Uddhav had not been able to become free of all these. Even the imagination of that moment which had been swaying Uddhav, how easily that moment had appeared in the company of Radha and passed away.... How meaningless was his bewilderment... Uddhav felt ashamed. Radha never even acknowledged that moment; a Krishna devoid universe, was never there for Radha...is not there...nor will ever be there....

By the contact of this universe of Radha, completely engrossed with Krishna, Uddhav's void and attachment both had peeled off like snake's skin. As Uddhav had left Gokul and proceeded towards Badri, he had become even lighter than air.

And this Badridham....

Walking with slow steps Uddhav cane and stood in front of the God installed in the sanctum of the Badri temple. He struck the gong of the temple bell and the peaks of the Himalayas resounded—Uddhav folded his hands and closed his eyes. In front of his closed eyes a silver line from a radiant light got imprinted. When he opened his eyes, in front was the glittering radiant Lord Badrinath.

A smile spread over Uddhav's lips.

This idol of Badrinath was made from touch-stone rock. By the touch of touch-stone any object could become gold. Uddhav felt that this extremely pure snow peak was not covered with snow but they were covered with gold. The waters of Alaknanda flowing near the feet was not melted snow; it was a stream of the flow of molten gold itself from the peaks.

Uddhav got goose-bumps. His every hair bloomed with joy. Were the rays of touch gold spraying from the idol bathing him also in gold?

What happened then? It was as if something flashed, Uddhav's eyes became steady. In place of the idol of Badrinath, he could see Krishna! The same peacock feather, same flute, the same world alluring, beyond time, compassionate smile and the universe pervading divine manifestation!

"Krishna!" the word broke out of Uddhav's lips. His eyes became moist. The Krishna idol in front became more and more hazy, as seen through the speedily flowing tears…and…and then? Did Krishna's lips twitch? Where did this sound come from? Where did the idol of Badrinath disappear?

"—Silence is the support for saying, Uddhav! Selfless deed is the support for the body! Praanayam is the support for the mind! He who dons these three supports, he is the real support holder, real ascetic! That desire which you are continually holding on to, by taking this asceticism you will be able to attain that formless entity O magnanimous Uddhav."

It was as if that rare knowledge of the words spoken by Krishna in his mansion at Dwaraka…was attained now… just now! Uddhav was standing silent for a long time. That intense desire of attaining the formless which Uddhav had been harbouring till today, that very same formless, i.e. the experience which he had a moment back, that gold bath—that touch of the touch-stone….

Uddhav drew his breath inside itself; closed his eyes—then he reminisced on all that which had become devoid of Krishna....

"Krishna!" he prayed mentally, "that deep touch which Radha got, the compassion of which experience this body was carrying till now, that very deep touch permeated within everyone...commencing with father Vasudeva till Kansa...within everyone's being.... O Achyuta! this indeed is the significance of your great departure...."

"Uddhav!" a sweet voice in a very gentle tone fell into his ears.

"Madhusoodan?" getting horipulation, Uddhav began staring at the snow clad peaks of Himalayas. It was as if the snow spread over the peaks was talking to Uddhav; he saw a slight movement in the eyes of Badrinath. Even the flow of Alaknanda and even the dawning morn over Vasudhaara remained still for a moment.

"Yes, Son!" again the same voice..."there is no Kansa in Krishna's mind...Nor Vasudeva..."

"What is this you...you...are saying, O Revered One?" this question arose from each and every hair of Uddhav, "putting father Vasudeva and Kansa...in the same category!"

"Yes, Son! For Krishna, each and every creature is only Radha, O Uddhav! that very contact with Radha's self-renunciation and surrender is, by itself supreme liberation..."

Uddhav understood—that nectar for which he was pining that itself is supreme liberation.... By the touch of Radha that day on the banks of Yamuna in Gokul, he had attained that...Krishna was indeed telling the truth—the moment Uddhav was able to comprehend Radha's self-renunciation, that very moment....

Uddhav was experiencing!—a sweet deep sleep was surrounding him! Taking a deep breath, he once again closed his eyes. In front of those closed eyes how many windows opened!

Beginning with Kansa and Shishupal, till Radha… how did these countless faces arise and manifest here? From where was this sound of flute arising? From where did the sound of the flute arise in the whizzing air of the Himalayas? Uddhav wished—how nice it would be if such sweet sleep never breaks…. The tune from the flute could be heard continuously.

"Uddhav.... You forgot my Son..." where did Krishna's voice come from, once more?

"—that joy which one gets in profound sleep (sushupti), such a state cannot be experienced in conscious state… However this does not mean that the deep sleep state is better in comparison to a 'conscious state'. This delusion… is after all Maya…. By understanding the inner soul, the covering of Maya disappears Son! Wake up and stand up O great soul!"

Uddhav opened his eyes with a start…. He experienced—that just like a speck in the supreme being, his existence was flying about somewhere…. A splendid solitude swallowing up the entire universe…a deep solitude in front was the idol of Badrinath…. It was as if the sound from the bell-gong which had arisen a short while back was even now imprinted on the snow clad peaks…. Everything was as it was before.

If so? What was it he had seen a moment ago? What had he heard?

Once again Uddhav stood in front of the idol with folded hands and head bent. And slowly came out of the temple. His mind had become very light…the mild push from the wind steered him towards the flow of Alaknanda…. Dashing against the stones rocks Alaknanda kept flowing with a vehement movement.

Uddhav looked at that vast water flow once; he cast his sight on the speed of its flow. He looked at the flow running towards the south. Are you standing on the banks of Alaknanda or in front of God Himself? Alaknanda continued to flow as it uses to flow always....

Uddhav dipped his feet in the flow. The coolness of the melting snow spread all over his body. Uddhav wanted to drown in that coolness. Sitting there on the banks itself he took bath.

He took one handful of water in his cupped palm from the flow. He held it for sometime and then again poured the handful into the Alaknanda. That handful also surrendered to that flow. Just a moment before, that handful of water which had a separate existence, once again united with that great flow and began running towards the eternal.

Uddhav bent his head.

It seemed as if the lofty peaks of the Himlayas showered snow arrows on his head! Uddhav continued standing and from his eyes...it seemed as if the Alaknanda's flow had burst out from it; the Himalayas appeared as if it had become light as flowers!

□□□